A Breath of Ecology
Musings from a Retreat Center

by

Sister Joel Gubler O.P.

DORRANCE
PUBLISHING CO
EST. 1920
PITTSBURGH, PENNSYLVANIA 15222

The contents of this work including, but not limited to, the accuracy of events, people, and places depicted; opinions expressed; permission to use previously published materials included; and any advice given or actions advocated are solely the responsibility of the author, who assumes all liability for said work and indemnifies the publisher against any claims stemming from publication of the work.

Dorrance Publishing Co
701 Smithfield Street
Pittsburgh, PA 15222
Visit our website at *www.dorrancebookstore.com*

ISBN: 978-1-4349-2888-7
eISBN: 978-1-4349-2240-3

Beginnings

In the 1950s, when I entered Rosaryville to begin my new life as a Sister, I felt the presence of my grandfather on these grounds, as he had been one of the Benedictine monks who founded a monastery here in the late 1800s.

They had come down by boat to Louisiana from Indiana and settled on higher ground about half a mile from the river where they had disembarked. They got to work constructing two three-story buildings, a cold storage, and various sheds, while digging a deep well that continues to furnish us with fresh water. They attempted to farm for their livelihood, were not successful, sold the property to the Dominican Fathers, and relocated.

Whenever I would wander into the old sheds, finding tools possibly left by the monks, I wondered which ones my grandfather might have used as a young seminarian (before he fell in love and married that young girl from New Orleans who used to visit friends across the road).

When the Dominican sisters purchased the property from the Fathers for a novitiate for young women, they raised and sold strawberries and operated a farm to help provide food for themselves. Now that the cows, pigs, chickens, strawberries, and house of formation are fading memories, Rosaryville has been established as a retreat center.

This place holds quite an interesting history.

Thoreau on Simplicity

As far back as 1845, Henry David Thoreau needed to get away from the materialistic world in which he lived in Concord, Massachusetts, as he felt most of the luxuries of life not only are not indispensable but also are positive hindrances to the elevation of humankind.

He borrowed an axe, went down to the woods by Walden Pond, and built his cabin to be alone with his beloved nature. In his journal, and later in a book titled *Walden,* he recorded his daily experiences of solitude among the small animals, his garden, and the pond.

How I can relate to this! Not to the building of a cabin, but the need for solitude and nature. Throughout my busy ministries in schools, parishes, and among the poor, I dreamed of my life as a gardener at our retreat center in my later years. And now it's happened.

Each evening, raccoons arrive at my hermitage from the woods knowing I have supper for them, and early in the morning the cats, goldfish, and birds await their breakfast, which I feel privileged to serve. During the day I tend to the flowers, bushes, and trees on our grounds.

Walden Pond and Rosaryville have gifted many throughout the years.

Animals Are a Gift

Animals, especially our pets, can really teach us how to live. Their love, faithfulness, forgiveness, trust, and patience are models for us.

We've often heard stories of courageous dogs who have saved lives, protected children, and warned of danger, yet people continue to speak of them as objects rather than subjects and think nothing of mistreating them. Although I'm really a dog person, in my situation here at the center, where dogs might bother retreatants, I can have only cats close by, but I have come to love them.

This past week my little female cat, Ernie, began to foam at the mouth, and of course I panicked and rushed her to the vet down the road. The vet found she had probably just eaten a frog and reminded me he had given her a rabies shot not long before. I had forgotten.

After being stuffed into a carrier and riding in a car to and from the clinic, both of which she hates, and being poked by the vet to get her temperature, Ernie finally arrived back home with me. As we later sat on the porch, she jumped into my lap, curled up, and went to sleep. Such forgiveness and unconditional love.

Yes, animals are certainly God's gift to us.

Spider Architects

Early this morning, between chapel prayers and breakfast, I grabbed a cup of coffee and walked toward the woods to enjoy nature at its peak, as I often do. While enjoying the cool air and birdsongs, I was stopped in my tracks by a remarkable scene: A spider web hung from one of the trees, low enough for me to examine it closely.

The web of a garden spider is marvelously intricate in construction and design to begin with, but the tiny droplets of dew clinging to it, reflecting the morning sun, gave it the appearance of diamonds on delicate lace. I stood mesmerized at the sight, realizing that a small spider had patiently and meticulously spun this architectural masterpiece of a web for hours.

Of course, its intentions may not have been necessarily to construct a thing of beauty but to trap its prey, with sticky threads woven right in the middle into which an innocent insect may fly.

I read that spider silk is the strongest natural fiber known; even steel drawn out to the same diameter is not as strong. Also, a scientist once stripped a spider in the American tropics of six feet of silk a minute, stopping after four hundred and fifty feet had been extracted. He said that the spider was capable of producing still more.

How much there is to learn about God's remarkable creatures.

Bringing Home the Beach

I love being able to enjoy the beach while sitting in my Adirondack chair miles away from the water.

All I have to do is put my channeled whelk shell up to my ear to hear the wind and waves of the seashore. In some mysterious way, there is always a certain movement of air inside the channel causing this. It's fascinating to enjoy it even on the beach itself.

The whelk is probably the most popular of all shells, half of it resembling a scroll. It definitely stands out among the collection on my nature shelf as the largest and the most artistically carved shell by God's hand.

When I walk in the sand along the shore of the Gulf Coast every Easter week during our spring camping trip, I am totally unaware of all the maritime life right under my feet. Crabs, worms, snails, sand dollars, flounders, and others exist safely down in the sand where they are cool and protected. Those living in the water are often washed up on shore, to our advantage and to the advantage of those who own souvenir shops in the area.

A bit of the seashore here surrounded by woods, a chapel, and flower gardens seems pretty idealistic to me.

Our Earth Deserves Respect

In 1979 Pope John Paul II named St. Francis of Assisi "patron of ecology," calling the saint an example of genuine and deep respect for the integrity of creation. Earth Day was first celebrated in San Francisco by his followers, the Franciscans, and now it's observed worldwide on the first day of spring.

The pope said what we all have to recover is a sense of enchantment, and too many people define the earth as material only, living in a world that's been stripped of its meaning; all have to understand the relationship of earth and humanity as a spiritual community.

While I care so deeply about preserving and enhancing the beauty of my surroundings as a gardener, I'm always conscious of the gravity of the careless depleting of our earth's resources without their being replenished.

Every newspaper, empty bottle, can, and plastic container I can collect finds its way to the local recycling center, as I do my small part with respect for the integrity of creation.

Lessons from Eagles

While driving not far from here, I looked up to find, to my surprise, a huge eagle's nest at the very top of a tall cypress tree. A bigger surprise later on, as I was returning home, was to see an eagle sitting on a branch right next to it, quite large and beautiful.

It's hard for me to believe it can live for seventy years! An interesting (and sad) fact is that at forty, its pointed beak curves inward, and its claws also curve inward and become soft. It can no longer grab its prey needed for food, and its wings are heavy with thick feathers that make flying difficult. It has to keep pecking hard until its beak wears off, and when it does, a new beak grows in its place and begins to pull out the old claws, which in turn pull out the old feathers.

How motivated these elegant birds, an emblem of our country's strength, must be to catch again the trade winds, soar above the earth, and continue to live for thirty more years. What an example for us when the going gets rough.

And to think Benjamin Franklin wanted the country's emblematic bird to be a turkey.

Slow-Moving Friends

When some of us go out to the wharf to feed the hungry occupants of our lake, we throw stale bread from the kitchen into the water, and the catfish and perch immediately grab it.

Because the turtles are so slow-moving, the fish usually beat them to the food. In fact, often when a turtle is lucky enough to catch some bread, a large catfish close by actually grabs it out of its mouth. Bullies.

Most species of turtles live in fresh water but can alternate between water and land. I don't ever see any of ours walking around the grounds, so I suppose they just stay in the lake and eat whatever is available in there—even bread now and then, if they're lucky.

All turtles lay their eggs on land, generally burying them or covering them with leaves. This I have yet to see. Unfortunately, animals such as raccoons, snakes, and large birds eat the eggs and hatchlings, and adults are not always immune despite their hard shells.

Some hawks will carry a turtle high into the air and drop it onto rocks to smash the shell. This I hope I never see.

Besides having the longest life span of all animals, the leatherback sea turtles may weigh as much as fifteen hundred pounds. I'm not sure about the hawks having any luck with those.

I just like to play with the little ones, about an inch and a half long, with little flowers painted on their shells.

Going Green

As we know, "going green" refers to maintaining a green, healthy planet on which to live. We say goodbye to millions of trees each day, and to oil, which is transformed into such commodities as plastic water bottles. We say goodbye, also, to clean air and water for drinking and growing food, as they are replaced by chemical pollutants.

I recall our family trips across the lake when I was a child, away from the city's carbon monoxide, when we suddenly began to inhale the strong aroma of pine as we approached the north shore. The clean air and water, which gifted this area, overtook us and continued to for those three years that we eventually lived there.

Materialism and excessive consumerism have overtaken so much of the population that we have forgotten the joy of living simply by cutting back, reusing, conserving, and enjoying the fact that the best things in life are free.

We can become impoverished in all that makes us human without the birds in flight, great forests, flowing streams, flowering fields, and the clouds and stars that grace our sky.

Amazing Ants

Have you ever heard of people apologizing to the ants as they poured poison on their hills? Yes, in fact, I do it. After all, I'm destroying the many chambers connected by underground tunnels used for nurseries, food storage, and resting places for the worker ants. Amazing creatures.

Ants have been living on Earth for more than 100 million years and can be found almost anywhere on the planet. There are about 20,000 different species of them.

When I first hang my hummingbird feeder from below the roof in the spring, I have to put a greasy substance on its top so the ants will not climb up the side of the house, down the long wire on which the feeder is hooked, and into the sugary substance.

Can you believe they can actually smell that sugar six feet above the ground? If we had such a powerful olfactory system, we could probably smell what's cooking at a restaurant a mile down the road.

Experiencing the Divine

As human beings, we can have a sense of the divine simply because of the magnificence of nature. Our senses become refined through the fragrance and indescribable beauty of song and movement in the world about us.

Children should be properly introduced to God's world in which they live: to the trees, food-bearing plants, flowers, birds and insects, the various animals, and the entire range of natural phenomena. We all have a need to be elevated beyond materialism.

Our naturalists, once simply romanticists, are now absorbing scientific data into their writings, and throughout North America, more than ten thousand ecologically oriented action groups have become a persuasive influence. They are found among the fields of economics, politics, education, and religion.

Advances in ecological activities can be observed throughout every continent, and in many countries, and in some of our states it is finally against the law not to recycle our natural resources, which are being drained from our planet.

How long will it take for everyone to get the message?

Busy as a Wasp

A few days ago, while in my favorite chair under the tree facing the woods, I saw a wasp fly under the armrest, but it didn't fly out. I thought, "Uh-oh, I wonder..." Sure enough, when I looked underneath, there it was, busy at work completing its nest.

It had progressed pretty far, and I saw some of the cells in the comb capped, which told me she already had laid eggs in there. How could I possibly destroy it? But how could I continue to sit there and risk being stung?

I had to leave for a few days, and when I returned the caps were off, and I saw little eyes at the top of each cell. The eggs had hatched and the mother wasp was nowhere in sight, so I pulled the little comb off the chair carefully where it was attached and laid it in the grass.

Since wasps, unlike honeybees, have no wax-producing glands, their hives/combs are paperlike substances made from chewed-up wood fibers. The mud daubers construct their combs from mud, usually on walls.

Solitary wasps work alone and don't build hives, while the social ones live in colonies numbering several thousand and construct homes for their eggs.

I hope this social one won't be too upset to find her babies in the grass and start searching for the culprit.

Bottled Water Safer?

W henever I'm shopping in grocery stores, it seems that one of the most popular items these days is bottled water, as I see customers loading cases of it into their shopping carts.

After doing a bit of research, I've found that bottled water is not safer than tap water, and about 40 percent of bottled water just happens to be plain municipal tap water after all. That same water is sold back by the water bottling companies to the public at thousands of times their cost.

About 1.5 billion gallons of oil a year (enough to run 100,000 cars) is used to make the plastic water bottles—only 10 percent of which are recycled; the rest end up in landfills.

So why don't we think about returning to those water pitchers in the fridge, coolers, and thermos bottles? This growth in our consumption of resources really cannot continue.

Life-Giving Trees

This morning, while I was enjoying sitting under a tree that I planted a few years ago, I lifted my face to the blue sky and after a few moments couldn't believe what I was experiencing.

A very delicate shower of droplets was falling on my face. Since there were no clouds in the sky, I knew it had to be coming from the leaves above me, and I sat still for a long time to enjoy this little unexpected miracle of nature.

When I went in later, I did some research and found that trees are constantly sending literally tons of water into our atmosphere from their leaves through the process of transpiration.

When I think of the beauty, shade, oxygen, and water that trees afford us (besides habitats and building materials), I recall the ending of a poem by Joyce Kilmer: "Poems are made by fools like me, but only God can make a tree."

Dressing Up the Pond

It took a few visits to aquatic stores, but I finally found water lilies for our pond that were not plastic. Imagine.

What a difference the presence of leaves and flowers make in the water, with the goldfish swimming in and out of them. Buoyant enough to support the weight of a frog, the lilies will pop up again if pushed down because of air cells in their leaves that keep them at the sunlit surface.

Plants on land have roots mainly for absorbing water and nutrients, and for anchoring themselves in place, but aquatic plants have hollow, air-filled pockets. Water lilies have all of their breathing pores located on the leaves' upper sides — a common adaptation in plants with floating leaves.

I read that the round Amazon water lily, six feet across, can easily support the weight of a child. A system of rigid, air-filled veins gives these huge leaves strength and buoyancy. One of these would fill my whole pond, blotting out the water and fish. I think I might rather have just a little plastic one floating around in there instead.

God Whispers

N o less incredible than the marvelous workings of the universe, which are far distances from us, is what we face in nature in our daily lives.

As I walk on our lovely grounds through the grass, I now and then stoop to pick a tiny wildflower, one of trillions that go unnoticed and even stepped on, and I examine it very closely. Each is an absolute masterpiece. The symmetrical shapes and colors under a magnifying glass can be framed for exhibit if enlarged. No human could create such a thing of beauty, perfection, and texture.

Our lives can consist of just shuffling along, doing what we have to do, when wonder and enchantment are ours for the asking and taking. I recall the words on a bookmark a friend once gave me that said the next time a sunset leaves us speechless and a garden of flowers takes our breath away, we should treasure the moment and in that silence listen as God whispers, "Do you really like it? I made it just for you."

Crowing of Roosters

A glorious sound to a city girl like me is a rooster crowing in the early morning out in the country.

During the week, while at a friend's home in the country, I suddenly heard crowing in the backyard and thought, "Doesn't that rooster know he's only supposed to do that when the sun rises?" Of course, later on I looked up some information on those majestic male chickens, also known as cocks.

The rooster usually is pictured in art as crowing at the break of dawn; however, he might crow at any time of the day. He is polygamous but cannot guard several nests of eggs at once, so he often sits on a high perch to serve as a lookout for his flock and crows to proclaim his territory. He will sound a distinctive alarm call if predators are nearby.

Jewish tradition in the Talmud refers to learning "courtesy from the cock," attributed to the rooster's behavior when he finds something good to eat: He calls his flock to eat first, and while giving this call, he repeatedly picks up a morsel of food and drops it to attract their attention.

What lessons we can learn from him.

The Plight of Our Planet

I recall one of my favorite spiritual books, which spoke of how we stand in awe at the stars splashed in such display across the heavens, at the shaping of the seas and the continents, at the tremendous cycles that lift huge quantities of water up from the seas and rain them down over the land. We marvel, also, at the numerous living forms in the sea and at bacteria in the soil from which life springs.

In another book on ecological spirituality, the author spoke of St. Francis of Assisi and St. Albert the Great, both of whom delighted in God's creations. In their day there was no capacity to inflict lasting damage to the balance of nature as there is today. During the past century, we have not simply continued to farm, mine coal, and spin cotton; we have found ways of controlling the forces that shape nature—the atom, the gene, gravity—while creating atomic fuel and weapons and bringing forth new life in laboratories through genetics.

How far will we dare to go before it's too late?

Ecological Endeavors

I felt blessed last weekend with two rewarding experiences.

First, I attended a meeting that introduced a community garden project, the goals of which are to provide our youth with the opportunity to grow food for community service and learn general concepts of working with and appreciating nature. A plot of donated land was being prepared for planting, with soil samples having been sent to the agricultural agency in order to purchase the necessary nutrients. We want our youth to know that food does not come from grocery stores, but from a miraculous process developed out of our earth.

Second, when I left the meeting with my car loaded with materials to be recycled, I found myself, as I turned in the gate, literally in a parade of cars heading for the large bin. It was a beautiful sight, and as we were all removing our cans, bottles, plastics, and newspapers from our cars, we were happily commenting on how more people were becoming aware of the necessity of recycling our natural resources rather than trashing them.

An appreciation of nature and care of our planet so often occupy my mind as I make daily efforts to do my share in these two areas here at our retreat center.

Beach Decorations

Last weekend, while basking in the sun and the roar of the waves at Gulf Shores, Alabama, I played beachcomber and collected seashells washed up on the sand.

As I sat and meditated on the colorful ones I had chosen, I thought about the fact that at one time there was life in those little shells. Those protective outer layers, or shells, were created by small animals and became part of their bodies. The shells are washed up on the shores empty and clean because the soft bodies inside have died, and some shells have split into two parts.

Unfortunately, the majority offered for commercial sale have been collected alive in bulk and then killed and cleaned. This large-scale exploitation has a strong negative impact on local ecosystems.

In tropical areas, there are far more species of colorful, large shells, but I love the nifty little ones I took home.

Restoring Our Resources

When a priest arrived here in Rosaryville not long ago to give a retreat, he brought with him several six-packs of bottled water. When he began to empty them, he asked if we recycled. I told him we do, and he said that if I had said no, he would have taken all the empties back with him a few hundred miles away to recycle. How encouraging to meet someone so serious about replenishing our natural resources.

The United States constitutes just 5 percent of the world's population and produces about 40 percent of the world's waste. Unfortunately, our rate of recycling is only about 28 percent.

Despite the education and awareness of global warming, climate change and the need to conserve Earth's precious resources, people continue to live as if there is no limit to them.

The Hershey Company produces about twenty million chocolate Kisses per day, using 133 square miles of aluminum to wrap them. Now, who is going to recycle those tiny wrappers?

Annually, 500 billion plastic bags are used worldwide. They are manufactured using oil, and it will take about five hundred years for them to decay in landfills. I read that in Los Angeles a ban on plastic bags is being seriously considered. New Zealand and other places in Europe already have banned them.

When I head for the store, my cloth bags are right beside me on the car seat to take in with me.

Color in Motion

Zinnias are great flowers that I plant every spring. Besides their various colors pleasing to the eye and their long life span during the summer months, butterflies love them. It seems the nectar in the flowers doesn't run out because day after day there they are, happily flitting around and enjoying their treat.

It's hard to believe those winged beauties were once caterpillars no one wanted around, as they constantly chewed through healthy plants in order to survive. Finally, they glued themselves to a leaf or branch, entombed themselves as a chrysalis, and began the process of becoming a thing of beauty.

I recall carrying a monarch butterfly chrysalis around for days when I was teaching science years ago, and when the moment of "resurrection" finally arrived, all the children in the schoolyard gathered around to experience the marvel of it slowly slipping out of its tomb.

When the wings finally had opened and dried off, the butterfly's long-awaited moment of freedom had arrived, and it flew off to start its new life.

When the time comes for them to migrate each year, monarchs actually are capable of flying from Mexico to southern Canada, a trip of approximately three thousand miles.

God's little creatures never cease to amaze me.

Our New Neighbors

I had to be very careful a few weeks ago while watering our Peace Garden. In one of our large flower pots, a mother wren had built her little nest, in the shape of an egg with the opening on its side.

Before I discovered it, I hosed the plant, and out shot the mother like a bullet. I was glad she hadn't yet laid her eggs and I hadn't disturbed her household. I was very cautious after that.

Not too long after, I heard the anticipated peeps and then watched the parents flying back and forth nonstop with worms and bugs in their bills. The little ones were soon out and flying from bush to bush, still being followed and fed by their parents. Finally, their stronger wings took them over the wall and out of sight: a sad day for those of us who had watched the whole process.

Wrens are small and rather inconspicuous, except for their loud and complex songs; they sometimes sing duets. I wonder if our wrens stayed in the nearby woods. I'm anxious to hear one of those duets.

Greenpeace

The blessed organization Greenpeace is a group fighting powerful corporations that are poisoning our air, water, and lands, increasing global warming, destroying our forests, pillaging aquatic life, and endangering human health. They use peaceful, confrontational campaigns targeting the corporate leaders and government policy makers.

God always sends help when His people utilize their faith and gifts. Prophets of the Old Testament courageously spoke out against injustice, relying on God's inspiration and support to bring about a better world.

Several years ago, after enjoying a three-month sabbatical focused on ecological spirituality, I settled here at our retreat center to care for the grounds and began to write a weekly article for the local newspaper on ecology. I had become aware of the area's lack of knowledge of the plight of our planet and the need for the recycling of its resources.

A wise Indian chief once said that we are simply borrowing this earth from our descendants and must protect it. How true, and sad, that is.

Discovering Delicacies

When friends from Quebec were visiting not long ago, they discovered something very valuable in our woods. They happen to be experts on mushrooms, and as I drove them around on the golf cart, what caught their eye was something I had seen very often but had just ignored as a poisonous parasite.

On the side of a tree was a clump of about three shelves of large, white mushrooms, fanning out from the bark close to the ground. My friends jumped out and headed to what they saw as a treasure and carefully picked them with a delicious meal in mind. Later, they sautéed them in butter and garlic, and I thought I was eating steak.

The mushrooms are of the polypores family and in Quebec (and maybe here too) are called "oyster mushrooms." I was told they are a common delicacy in the homes of Italians in the area. I'm not Italian, but I will certainly be on the lookout now for more of these treats on our trees.

Our Feathered Friends

F eathers lying here and there on our property are a common sight. We have wild turkeys on the ground and birds in the air, not to mention those at the feeders and in the birdbath.

We find feathers in all sizes and colors, from hummingbirds to herons and even the ducks that enjoy our lake sometimes. Those little hummingbirds have about 940 feathers, while the largest number has been found on swans: a whopping 25,000!

Birds keep their feathers clean by preening, that is, by rubbing the beak over an oil gland at the base of the tail. Using the beak as an applicator, the bird spreads the oil over a patch of feathers and then runs the feathers through its beak, nibbling as it goes. This straightens them and removes any dirt particles. Our herons, however, are lacking oil glands, so they preen with the fine powder produced by specialized powder-down feathers.

Although feathers of many birds are beautiful to behold, their practical purposes are to enable the bird to fly and to insulate, allowing survival in bitter cold weather.

Although tough and resilient, feathers fray and wear out with use and periodically must be shed. Growing new feathers takes energy, and molting must be synchronized with periods when the birds are not involved in such strenuous tasks as breeding or migrating.

On my nature shelf I have several different feathers I have found here in the past few years. I marvel at their construction and at the various colors in each. They're next to my amazing seashell collection.

The best things in life are free.

Our Green Pond

I flood our goldfish pond every week, put in drops of algae destroyer every day, put in plants to give off oxygen, but, by George, here comes that algae again, even after I've used a broom to try to remove it.

I could put a dozen algae-eaters in there, but they'd be an awful-looking sight stuck all over the sides. What to do?

The green, slimy algae that those of us with fish ponds are constantly fighting is actually considered a type of bacteria, and even though the water itself is crystal clear and our fish look happy, the pond looks polluted with that green clinging to the concrete.

I suppose the sun beating down on it all day doesn't help matters, as the algae love to bask in it, and we can't plant a tree near the pond because it's surrounded by flagstones.

The Latin word "algae" means "seaweed." One type can grow several hundred feet long. That's okay out in the ocean. I'll just keep tolerating the fuzz and strings that keep growing out of the sides and bottom of our pond. Anyway, I see the fish nibbling on it now and then. Maybe it's a treat for them.

What's Happening to Our Food?

In a book I'm reading about what's on the shelves in our supermarkets, I'm realizing that often our nation's weight problems and poor health are not necessarily our fault. More and more, marketers are adding new types of preservatives, fats, sugars, and other food substances to our daily meals.

Since the 1960s manufacturers have been baking with—and restaurants have been frying with—something called trans fat. It's cheap and effective in preserving food and making it tastier and crisper, but it increases our risk of heart disease.

In the 1970s food manufacturers, looking for a cheaper ingredient to replace sugar, came up with a substance called high fructose corn syrup. Today this fattening ingredient is found in an unbelievable array of our foods.

Due to farmers' efforts to achieve higher yields and plants that grow faster, the plants aren't able to make or take in nutrients at the same rate, and six out of thirteen nutrients show major declines.

As I continue to read this book, I feel it should be placed on a shelf in the Horror Stories section of a bookstore, and I hope the farmers eventually go back to the old-fashioned way of raising crops for the health of our country.

Venus the Beautiful

All those who rise very early as I do get the treat before daybreak of being greeted by the brightest object after the sun and moon up in the eastern sky: Venus. Although a planet, it is known as the Morning Star and was named by the ancients after their goddess of beauty.

Venus is slightly smaller than Earth, but its rotation is very slow; 243 Earth days equal one Venus day. Although it is lovely to behold, it is probably the least hospitable place for life in the solar system.

Its several layers of thick clouds are composed of sulfuric acid, and the surface temperature is hot enough to melt lead. It probably once had water, but it all boiled away and is now quite dry. It is about 800 million years old and is still volcanically active.

Never mind all of that; it's really a beautiful sight to behold early in the morning and again in the evening in the western sky after Earth has continued to orbit toward the east.

A Sight for Sore Eyes

A few days ago, I hit the brakes as I drove under the arch at our entrance. In front of me was a magnificent double rainbow, and I couldn't move as I was so struck by its beauty.

The pattern of colors is always the same in the spectrum: red, orange, yellow, green, blue, indigo, and violet; however, in the second rainbow, the colors were reversed.

When I told a friend about this meteorological phenomenon I witnessed, she informed me that she once saw a rainbow actually circling the sun! I've seen an aura of light circling the moon at night, but didn't know that rainbows did that too. This I would love to see.

Pots of gold at the end or not, money could never buy such a God-given gift.

Cute but Pesky Squirrels

While in California during the summer visiting friends, I encountered quite a few flowers, bushes, and trees I had never seen before. A sight with which I was very familiar, however, was that of squirrels jumping from tree to tree in their backyard.

There was one squirrel in particular who visited every morning when it was time for its breakfast. I had been told about it, and while meditating on their comfortable back porch that first morning, I looked up from my book and saw that little bushy-tailed visitor, just sitting there motionless and staring me down for the longest time.

I knew what I had to do to be able to continue my praying, so I found the jar of peanuts and fed it right from my hand. It was a new experience for me, as I never had met one so friendly.

They're cute little things but can be a menace at times, such as when they devoured every new leaf on the banana trees I had planted by our patio. After trying every means I could think of to get rid of them, I finally surrendered and dug up the trees.

They are found in most countries, as they can live in climates ranging from tropical rainforests to deserts. They can vary in size from three inches long to twenty-one inches long, and in weight from five ounces to fourteen pounds. Their large eyes give them excellent vision.

I guess I'll just have to learn to tame one around here and get a large supply of peanuts. Or maybe not.

Armadillo Woes

Not long ago I saw an armadillo lying very still on our sidewalk, so I presumed he was dead. A little while later he had changed positions, and when it started to rain he was gone. My heart went out to him, and I hoped he wasn't suffering. I then found myself forgiving him for all the plants he had turned over in our garden during the nights.

My sympathy disappeared when, the next morning, I found chaos in my garden again. Of course, it could have been a relative of his. The red pepper to ward them off worked until the rain came. I then sprinkled moth balls all over the garden, and things were still intact the next morning; of course, the white balls all over the place looked a little ridiculous.

Although ferocious looking, those armored mammals really are not aggressive. When danger threatens, they try to hide by burrowing quickly into the ground, and in an emergency, they resort to rolling themselves up into a ball, completely protected by their hard outer shell.

I'm really glad I don't live in Brazil, where they grow to be four feet long and weigh over a hundred pounds. I surely could forget about the pepper and mothballs then.

Our Amazing Trees

I have to say one of the most fascinating experiences of nature for me is viewing a leaf with the sun filtering through it.

I sit in my comfortable Adirondack chair under the tree behind my little house, look up at the thousands of leaves arched above me, and then focus on a single leaf.

The intricate system of tiny veins carrying water to every section of the leaf is miraculous. Then there's the thought of the process of it getting there. It begins in the roots of the tree, and then defying gravity, travels up the trunk into each branch, ultimately distributing the water evenly into the thousands of leaves.

When we look at a leaf we see one flat level, when actually it's structured in four levels. The top is a thin waterproof coat; under that is a layer of transparent cells lying over tightly packed cells containing chlorophyll. In the bottom spongy layer are loosely arranged cells where water and gases can move freely.

We don't have to search far to discover miracles. We can look in our own backyard.

Those Stinky Little Bugs

Not long ago I found a stinkbug on one of my tomato plants and knocked it off, letting it know in no uncertain terms that it wasn't welcome in my garden here. A few days later, a friend of mine informed me that I should have left it there, as it eats other unwanted insects.

Then, of course, I decided to do some research on those little fellows and discovered that no, I really don't want them around—for a couple of reasons.

First of all, there's that aroma. Stinkbugs got their name from the scent glands located on their abdomen and thorax. Their scent is always slightly apparent, but if you smash them or get them pulled into your vacuum cleaner, look out.

Second, they're quite accomplished at feeding on fruits and vegetables, a habit that is very upsetting to gardeners and especially to farmers whose harvests become unmarketable as fresh products. The bugs can really get around, too. They're found in twenty-six of our states and in thirty-seven other countries.

So, even if stinkbugs are nice enough to eat other unwanted insects, go ahead and flick them or spray them off. Just don't make the mistake of stepping on them.

Majestic Pines

The most numerous trees to grace our extensive grounds are the short- and long-leaf pines, reaching approximately 100 to 150 feet into the air. They have earned a special place in our hearts with their fresh scent, their soft humming as wind blows through their branches, their majestic beauty, and their cones, which we gather for bonfires and sell for decorations.

They may not compare with the 275-foot-tall sequoias with trunks 32 feet in diameter and life spans of 3,000 years, but they are valuable trees, yielding timber for a variety of uses such as telephone poles and paper pulp and acting as an important source of turpentine.

Pollination takes place when wind blows pollen from male to female cones. The green female cone becomes brown and woody, its scales spreading apart and dropping their winged seeds, which usually take off with the wind.

As a child in the city, it was with the aroma of pine now and then that I was transported to the woods, as our family crossed the lake into the Ozone Belt—Land of the Pines for a week of vacation during the summer.

Never did I dream when I was twelve years old that we would actually move up there among those majestic trees.

Singing Praise of Our Planet

AUTHOR: Can you provide the name of this composer/singer? Since you are quoting her songs, it would be fair to give her credit.

While attending an ecology convention last year, we were all entertained on the last night by an amazing composer and singer whose music could change the world. This young woman has written numerous songs that teach important messages about sustainable living, recycling, eco-activism, sacred ecology, and simple living. Her name is Joyce Rouse and she calls herself, "Earth Mama." Her CDs portray a serious message while exhibiting a sense of humor. For example, in respect for animals one line goes, "That juicy little burger once had a mama like you, who roamed around the pasture before it became your shoe."

In reverence for the earth: "Who makes diamonds? Who makes gold? Who is wondrous to behold?"

Concerning the unnecessary stuff we accumulate: "I have mittens for a kitten and don't even have a cat; I will never be a cowboy, but I have a cowboy hat."

A plea for simplicity: "Choose a little, use it a lot, and only take what you need."

I would love to put at least one of her CDs in every classroom to give the students an awareness of the beauty, sacredness, and plight of our planet Earth as they sing, clap, and dance to the music.

Consumed with Consuming

An article I read lately stated that human beings have used more raw materials since World War II than in all previous recorded history. The ability to produce as fast and cheaply as possible has ruined countrysides and abused people and animals.

According to a recent survey, the United States, which once was considered to have the happiest citizens in the world, is now number twenty-three on the list. All the billions of barrels of oil and millions of acres of trees it took to create our material progress seems not to have moved the satisfaction meter an inch.

When the garbage truck arrives here in the morning I just want to throw all the glass, cans, plastics, and newspaper in with the rest of the waste and be done with it. But I can't. I know that in years to come, if I'm up in heaven looking down on a desolate planet devoid of trees and natural resources, I'll be able to say, "I'm innocent. I didn't cooperate in any of that indifference and destruction that resulted in this."

Guess I'll just keep on collecting, bagging, storing, and hauling, and dumping at the recycling centers in spite of the trouble it entails.

Honey's Many Properties

Several times while shopping for food, I have seen large wire containers on the floor filled with bottles of honey, as though it were some surplus, unimportant commodity needing to be bought and taken away.

When I use honey, I see every drop as a precious form of food that has been collected and enjoyed for thousands of years, produced exclusively by bees and unable to be substituted. Honey is mentioned often in the Bible for its rich and savory properties and for its use as a treatment for a variety of ailments. Ancient Greeks associated lips anointed with honey with the gift of eloquence.

International food regulations state that "honey stipulates a pure product that does not allow for the addition of any other substance," and history knows examples of honey preservation for centuries. This is due to the bees fanning the nectar in the hive to evaporate much of its water, an act that prevents fermentation.

Observing the life and activities of bees is a study that opens your eyes to the marvels of God's little creatures.

Recycling Isn't Fun

Lately, after collecting from several friends lots of bags of old newspapers that filled the car trunk and backseat, I knew the worst was yet to come. I pulled up to the big recycling Dumpster next to a school and started lifting those heavy bags.

The weather was hot, the opening of the dumpster was very high, and the papers were difficult to shake out of the bags, and I thought I'd never come to the end of that ordeal. All the while, however, I kept thinking, "It's worth it. It's worth it."

When I think of the millions of trees cut down every day for papermaking, I actually feel weak because I know it takes three tons of trees to make one ton of paper. I have such a respect and love for trees that I've planted them wherever I have lived and continue to do so here on our grounds. I have to admit that I plant the fast-growing kind so I can enjoy their beauty and shade. I never have planted one of those live oaks that take years and years to develop.

Because of the oxygen our trees provide, scientists speak of them as "the lungs of the earth." I always try to remember to breathe deeply when under a tree, knowing that my own lungs will benefit from it.

A Little Berry That's Blue

A few days ago I bought a bag of frozen blueberries and was so shocked at how high-priced they were that I went to a nursery and bought my own blueberry bush to plant next to my house. That'll show 'em.

Blueberries are native to North America, and Michigan is the leading producer, having harvested as much as 490 million pounds in one year—32 percent of those grown in our country.

Several towns in Maine, however, claim to be the blueberry capital, and the berry is often as much a symbol of Maine as the lobster, with the state's crop requiring about fifty thousand beehives for pollination. (Wow!)

Blueberries are the largest fruit crop in Canada, with Nova Scotia in the lead.

The lowbush blueberry plant averages about ten inches in height, and the highbush berry plant averages as high as thirteen feet.

Blueberries possess antioxidants, which help maintain normal blood pressure and control the spread of cancer, Alzheimer's, and urinary tract infections.

Pesticides that would impede their nutritional value are a significant concern in production, so it might be a good idea to get over to a nursery soon and plant a few blueberry bushes in your yard, too.

Of Beauty and Song

A group of bird-watchers spent the day on our grounds not long ago and were amazed at the number of species of birds they found. I don't know how many we have, but I read that in our state of Louisiana alone there are about 428 species, despite the cleared forests, shrunken wetlands, saltwater intrusion, and oil exploration.

Unfortunately, the many species that John Audubon, lover and painter of birds in this state of Louisiana, saw in abundance either are extinct or never will be seen again in such abundance. Nevertheless, several million birds still pass through this area during the migratory season on their way to South America, making a flight of more than five hundred miles over the water.

I really hope those serenading me in the mornings don't have plans to head farther south any time soon.

A Cherry Tomato's Surprise

While visiting a friend in California a few months ago, I picked a cherry tomato and put it in a plastic bag to take back home to plant.

When I returned, I simply dropped the tomato on a small plot of soil, and within a week or so there was a little mass of about twenty seedlings coming up.

After carefully separating them into individual containers to plant and distribute to other garden lovers, I put several seedlings in our enclosed patio, where the raccoons couldn't get to them.

What a delight to watch the healthy growth and blossoms from that one small tomato, far removed from its California sun.

The enjoyment of finally picking and eating the ripened crop while marveling at the miracle of it all was quite an experience.

Examining Our Values

How heartbreaking it is for those of us who have long cherished our precious trees in this rural area to witness the destruction of many of them for the purpose of new housing developments within view of our property.

Housing developments and paper manufacturing seem to be the major causes of the destruction of our forests, but in the rain forests of Brazil, for example, the loss seems to stem from another industry—hamburgers.

Many of that country's poor have been displaced from their homes by ranchers and loggers, while valuable forests are cleared to provide land for cattle to graze in order to supply those hamburger places Americans so often frequent.

Seventy-four-year-old Sister Dorothy Stang recently was killed by gunmen hired by ranchers as she persisted in defending the poor and their rain forests.

As the population of vegetarians increases in this country, so will the preservation of oxygen and habitation of those forests, along with healthier and thinner Americans.

Remarkable Roses

Arosebush that had been given to me as a gift a few years ago just up and died this week. Within three days it was gone. No explanation. Of all the rosebushes in our Peace Garden, this one was my favorite. I had cut many beautiful pink buds from it and loved its light scent.

I dug it up when I was sure there was no life left in it and headed straight to the nursery for a rosebush to plant in its place. I couldn't find one like it, as it had been a hybrid from the agricultural center of our nearby university. The new one would have to do, and I'd give it as much love as I had given the other.

The cultivation of roses began in the Orient, and its popularity spread throughout Europe, furthering the flower's role in symbolism, religion, and art. The red rose, especially, has been a symbol of caring and love. Luxury-minded Greeks reclined on beds of rose petals, and to this day "a bed of roses" is the epitome of ease.

My father always grew roses, and I recall as a child taking small bouquets of them to school for the altar in our classroom, sniffing that wonderful aroma all the way there. How unfortunate that laboratories have removed so much of that unique perfume from such an endearing, exquisite flower.

The Gift of Cows

We no longer have cows here on our grounds, but luckily, right across the road from us, a small herd grazes throughout the day. It's not only a peaceful sight but also a useful resource for our gardens; all I have to do is cross over with buckets and help myself to all the manure I want. The farmer, of course, is our friend.

Don't turn your nose up. There are lots of droppings that have been sitting out there for a long time in the sun, have no odor, and have the consistency and weight of papier-mâché. They contain no chemicals harmful to our garden—only grass that has gone through a cow.

Besides grinding up most of the manure and mixing it with the soil, I fill up a large sack with it and put it down into a barrel of water. After a few days of soaking, the water becomes "manure tea," which I scoop up to pour on the plants.

I read that more than 100 million pounds of chemicals are dumped on U.S. lawns and gardens each year. We don't want to be a part of that.

Scary Owls

I find it a little eerie at night to hear the *hoot, hoot, hoot* of an owl deep in our woods. It sounds so forlorn. No wonder owls are steeped in the legend, art, and folklore of nearly every culture.

Owls have humanlike features, as their eyes are located at the front of the head rather than at the sides like other birds. They are superb at detecting prey, and their hunting is very silent because their wings are fringed, muffling the noise of air passing through them as they approach their victims.

There is an association between owls and misfortune that stems perhaps from the fact they are nocturnal and nighttime often is equated with evil.

Although I've only heard the hooting sound of our owls out here, they also can whistle, shriek, chatter, and growl. Perhaps I've heard those other sounds in the woods but didn't identify them with an owl.

I have yet to see one. If we have a great horned owl out there, it's more than two feet tall and capable of seizing and killing small animals. That's not a very happy thought for me, knowing my three cats are outside at night.

Moonstruck

I t's not easy for me to get up from my chair outside and go inside on the nights of a full moon. We're given this treat every four weeks as the moon completes its orbit around the earth. The moon, Earth's only natural satellite and nearest neighbor in space, is actually about one-fourth the size of Earth and usually about 240,000 miles away.

There are times we are somewhat startled by the gigantic size of a full moon rising above the horizon. The moon appears huge when its orbit, not being a perfect circle, brings it 25,000 miles closer to Earth than when it's at its farthest point.

A full moon, another one of God's gifts, always has afforded a romantic setting in movies and in paintings, and I can recall playing volleyball as a teenager on the beach at night, bathed in its light and awed by its reflection on the white sand.

Something Wrong with This Picture

While billions of dollars a year are spent in this country on weight-loss programs, two-thirds of the world goes hungry every day. What's wrong with this picture?

I noticed one hamburger place advertising not only quarter-pounders but also third-pounders, a thicker burger with more fat and calories to add to the obesity prevalent in our country. Obesity, coupled with a lack of exercise due to televisions and computers, is leading this country in the wrong direction. Unfortunately, a great deal of this problem is found in children, our hope for the future.

Nutritionists tell us we should eat three meals a day. It's not how much, but *what* we eat, that keeps us well. Three healthy meals probably can equal the calories in just one of those whopping cheeseburgers with fries.

Having worked with the poor in Mexico for several years, I know poverty firsthand and can't help comparing our abundance and waste of food with their lack of it.

I treasure the food I pick from my organic garden because I know it's healthy and that even large portions are not fattening.

Songs of Birds

This morning at daybreak I heard two birds, far off in the woods, calling back and forth to each other for several minutes—not singing, but using call notes.

Songs are not their only language. They use call notes to communicate, scold, call young, beg for food, and keep together as a flock. I wondered what those two were saying to each other.

In nearly all bird species, males are the more impressive songsters. They sing primarily to establish a claim to a territory, and some repeat their songs thousands of times a day. Most birds sing in the morning or evening and are quiet during the middle of the day.

There's a mockingbird that sings its repertoire every morning around the same time in the large oak tree behind the chapel. Ornithologists have recorded mockingbirds actually imitating at least thirty species of birds, as well as the sounds of other animals and the sounds of machines.

By tradition, the bird with the most beautiful song is the nightingale. I'll have to ask the bird-watchers in this area if there are any of those around. I hope so.

Lighting Up the Night

When I was a child, summer nights brought about a world of enchantment for us all—old as well as young. We went outside and viewed with awe, chased, and caught in jars (temporarily) those beautiful, soft-winged beetles called fireflies, or lightning bugs, which sparkled around the whole neighborhood.

The light, or bioluminescence, of the males is twice as bright as that of the females and serves the purpose of attracting mates. It seems all of God's creatures have a way of doing that.

Those blinking taillights usually start flashing at dusk and stop by midnight. Different species time their flashes differently to help ensure that only members of the same species respond by flashing back. Amazing.

God thought of so many ways to make our stay on this earth as delightful as possible. By day our grounds sparkle with color, while at night they sparkle with lights.

Range of Birds

Our retreat center is home to various types and sizes of birds. I can identify only a few of their songs and calls, but I enjoy all of their sounds—even that of the turkeys.

I know it's daybreak when I hear the cardinal sing, and a little later I hear the mockingbird across the way start its repertoire of mocking all the others.

It's obvious that a lot of birds come together to devour the seeds in the feeder because every time I check, it's absolutely empty. They do their eating in silence.

Although extinct now, the moa bird of New Zealand reached a height of ten feet and weighed half a ton. Imagine keeping a feeder filled for one of those. Some of their well-preserved eggs occasionally are discovered in swamps and found to weigh about twenty pounds with a circumference of three feet.

I'll just continue to keep my little birds happy while they, in turn, keep me entertained.

Fearful Neighbors

One day I saw some of our workmen standing around a pickup truck behind the workshop and seriously looking down into the back of it. As I slowly and cautiously allowed myself to peek in, I couldn't believe my eyes. Curled up and filling the entire back of the truck was the largest alligator I had ever seen.

Since alligators can be dangerous, a man from the Wildlife and Fisheries Department was called to remove this specimen from our lake. The gator was shot and was on his way to being converted into alligator stew.

Alligators come out of our swamp between the river and our buildings, and they enjoy floating in the lake during the hot months. Usually they're small, and they remain out in the middle of the water without bothering anyone.

My little hermitage is at the edge of the woods, and after seeing what was living in the area I became a little nervous about sitting back there, wondering if at any moment one of those monsters would appear and head toward me.

One morning I heard a sound close by much like a cow would make and was afraid it might be an alligator. I went to a nearby alligator farm, inquired about the sounds alligators make, and for some reason, none of the workers knew. Later, I was near a pond a few miles away and heard the same sound. Guess what? It was a bullfrog. Bull-cow: same sound. You learn something new every day.

I'm still a little nervous sitting back there.

Marshes and Swamps

While visiting a retreat center in South Carolina not long ago, I was able to experience low and high tides firsthand. The building in which I stayed was at the edge of an extensive area of marshlands, a short distance from the ocean, where two daily high and low tides took place.

I sat on the screened porch with some of the other Sisters who spoke of how marshes are critically important wildlife habitats, serving as breeding grounds for a wide variety of animal life, especially ducks and geese.

As we know here in Louisiana, a marsh is different from a swamp, which has a greater proportion of open water surface dominated by trees rather than grasses and is home to alligators, turtles, raccoons, and other water-loving animals and birds.

I enjoy visiting our Louisiana swamps, with picturesque cypress trees, cascading moss, white herons, and little cabins with their boats of hollowed-out logs, called pirogues, sitting in the water nearby.

Amazing Rain

I sat by my window overlooking the woods for quite a while yesterday, caught up in the miracle of rain giving new life to our plants and trees. I imagined the goldfish in the pond were enjoying it also. I only hoped the rainy days wouldn't end when spring arrived and I had my vegetable garden plowed up for another organic crop.

It's interesting to know that all clouds are composed of billions of tiny water droplets and ice crystals, yet even though they all may contain several tons of moisture, many of them pass by without producing so much as a shower.

Conditions have to be right for a rainfall. When the droplets have collected bits of dust and have continued to collide with each other, they gradually grow heavier and larger until finally gravity pulls them down as rain.

Miraculously, each drop falls separately, and although picking up momentum as they fall, they can hit the earth so gently as not to break a petal of a flower or a blade of grass. Another of nature's miracles.

Food for the Gods

Last week when I drove up to my sister's house, I was met with an unexpected surprise. There were her two enormous fig trees absolutely loaded with that beautiful, ripe fruit. Unfortunately for her, but lucky for me, she and her husband were leaving for Europe the next day for two weeks.

I loaded up several bags and buckets with figs, and when I returned home, I got down to the business of making them into preserves to sell in our gift shop. I returned to my sister's the next day for more figs and placed more preserves on the shelves to sell. They were gone in a few days.

Figs, which are very common in our area, are practically unknown to those in northern states, as they are native to warm regions such as southwest Asia and the Mediterranean. In fact, they are mentioned often in the Bible as one of the most common and valuable foods of those early times.

The commercial production of figs is in dried form, since the ripe fruit, once picked, does not keep or transport well. In any form, figs are one of the best plant sources of calcium, fiber, magnesium, potassium, and vitamin K.

The prophet Muhammad is quoted as saying about the fig, "If I had to mention a fruit that descended from paradise, I would say this is it." I agree.

Those Marvelous Nests

Anyone who has had the opportunity and privilege to watch a bird construct its nest can't help but feel a sense of awe at the power of its instincts, determination, and perseverance—not to mention the masterpiece of its finished product.

Nests throughout the world differ in shape, size, and location. Some are shallow depressions in sand, knotholes of branches, burrows in the ground, chambers in trees, piles of vegetation, mud domes with entrance tunnels, and woven sacks.

I once observed the entire process of nest building, followed by the incubation period, the hatching, and the feeding, that took place in a tree right outside my window. The intricacy and stability of the nest securely held the mother bird, who patiently protected her eggs through sun, wind, and rain as the father bird faithfully brought her food.

After seeing the hatching, the constant care by both parents, and finally the empty nest, I couldn't help but feel depressed at their departure yet grateful for having been able to witness such an event.

Rain and Tree Frogs

From the looks of all the rapid growth of my plants after a rainfall, compared to after a hosing, I've discovered that our well water obviously is not the same as that pure, blessed rain from the clouds. How wonderful to have the heavens water our gardens while I get other chores done around here.

I'm not the only one who enjoys that treat; so do those little green tree frogs with those amazing suction cups on their feet clinging to the sides of the buildings. It seems they can't get enough rain, and they let the heavens know about it. By sending air over their vocal cords, their bleat resonates in sacs puffed out from their throat. I suppose they're part of that chorus out there in the woods at night, and I'm sure they're the loudest.

I've never heard such a loud noise come from such a tiny creature.

Fun with Clay

My latest project is molding from clay sculptures of little critters who are at home on our grounds—in the trees, in the woods, in hollowed-out stumps, in the lake, and in the open fields.

My little clay birds, raccoons, squirrels, alligators, fish, possum, and deer are decorated with bright colors and flowers and have comical faces and poses. They are purchased in our gift shop as pencil holders.

During the process of molding and fashioning these articles, I am amazed how creative an endeavor this is: transforming common clay from Mother Earth into lifelike statuettes and endless other items.

I always marvel at the abundance of resources we constantly receive from this, our planet, to sustain, fulfill, and even amuse us.

Our Valuable Worms

Within our planet's diverse animal kingdom we find the following superlatives and statistics:

- Longest life span: Turtle—160 years
- Largest: Blue Whale—90 feet long
- Smartest: Chimpanzee & Dolphin
- Fastest: Cheetah—70 mph
- First to have a muscular system: Worm

Speaking of the lowly worm, who lives underground, I wonder if I'm the only one in the world who apologizes, almost tearfully, to a worm I accidentally chop in two with a shovel. I was told they continue to live, and while researching that possibility, I came across the following facts about earthworms—of which, by the way, there are more than two thousand species.

Earthworms act as living plows. On an acre of good soil, they can bring as much as eighteen tons of subsoil to the surface each year. They do this by eating their way through the earth, digesting its contents of dead leaves and other organic material. Their constant mixing and loosening of the upper layers of the soil permits air to penetrate and water to percolate through, thus improving the ground as a living place for plants.

It's exciting for me to uncover those little red, plump creatures, which are so helpful in the garden as they function in silence and in the dark. I'm still not sure if they continue to live after my unintentionally hacking them. I hope so, and really think it's okay to continue to be such a softie when it comes to animals and insects.

Our Charming Turkeys

From our woods wild turkeys come strutting every day, some elegantly spreading their tail feathers, others sounding out their gobble-gobbles, which are heard throughout our grounds. At times, I've counted more than twenty in a group as they searched for small, tender plants (such as those in our garden, unfortunately), and seeds.

Although wild turkeys are not as large as those raised on farms, the males weigh up to twenty-five pounds, and the females weigh around ten pounds. They roost in the trees at night, away from predators. During the day the males strut around, attempting to attract the females by spreading their tail feathers now and then, peacock style.

The turkeys are so large that I didn't know they could fly very high until my cat Timmy chased one, and it flew to the top of a tall pine tree. In fact, I discovered they can fly an estimated forty to forty-five miles an hour over short distances and cover more than a mile while airborne.

In late April the females leave the flock and find nesting spots in the woods, laying one egg nearly every day until her nest contains an average of twelve eggs. In twenty-eight days the babies arrive.

Thank God the government began passing hunting laws to protect turkeys in the early 1900s, when they nearly became extinct. I can't imagine our center without them adding to the beauty of the grounds.

Picky Bluebirds

I've always heard songs and read poems and stories about bluebirds, but I don't think I've ever actually seen one in person (in bird?) until a few months ago. Father Hank, a nature lover from a nearby parish, set up several houses for them here in Rosaryville, and now every time I ride toward the barn in the golf cart near their houses, out fly little birds with feathers in a really beautiful shade of blue. It's quite a sight to behold.

Bluebirds won't live in just any house; the dimensions have to be just right. Houses should be mounted about four to five feet above the ground, near open fields and water sources. Since about 80 percent of their diet consists of insects, bluebirds need to be able to spot them in the grass and swoop down on them. The entrance should be a hole one-and-a-half inches in diameter and six inches above the floor, and the house should contain an air vent on the ceiling and a drain hole on the floor.

Yes, bluebirds are picky.

Forests Won't Last Forever

There's such a feeling of satisfaction in watching the growth of a tree that you yourself have planted. Our woods are filled with leafless trees in the spring, and I have dug up several to plant in conspicuous places to enhance the beauty of our grounds. I even speak to them and touch them in their beginning stages.

I just read an article about a young man who hiked through the Sierra Nevada and Cascade mountain ranges and returned with photos of stripped forests left only with stumps as far as the eye could see. The forests and the many animals it had sheltered had been gouged from the earth.

I learned a local printing company uses about half a million sheets of paper every two months for their business. There are hundreds of thousands of these companies, as well as schools and offices that use paper—a product of trees—on a very large scale.

I have worn a path to the recycling center and will continue to do so with carloads of used papers to do my part in conserving our trees.

Our Remarkable Universe

While on sabbatical a few years ago at a retreat center in South Carolina, I attended a three-month art and spirituality program emphasizing the creative and dynamic role of the human in an unfolding universe.

In two parts, I want to list the scientific account of God's creative evolving of our universe, beginning with billions of years before the birth of Christ:

- 13.7 billion years—The universe flared forth out of ultimate mystery.
- 12 billion—Stars and galaxies were formed.
- 4.5 billion—Our solar system and sun were born.
- 4.3 billion—The moon lit up the night sky.
- 3.9 billion—Photosynthesis occurred: Microbes captured light for nourishment, and oxygen was released.
- 2 billion—Single-celled life breathed oxygen, and the ozone layer was formed.
- 1 billion—Simple cells joined for survival and development, and sexual reproduction began.

Our Remarkable Universe, Part Two

God's creative evolving of the universe between 700 million and 2.6 million years before the birth of Christ:

- 700 million years—Multicellular life formed; ecosystems emerged.
- 600 million—Nervous systems and sight evolved.
- 510 million—Backbones formed in fish to protect nervous systems.
- 425 million—Water life moved onto land; trees appeared.
- 390 million—Insects emerged and took flight.
- 300 million—Coal deposits formed; forests and amphibians evolved.
- 235 million—Reptiles evolved from amphibians; dinosaurs ruled.
- 210 million—Land mass broke into continents; mountains and oceans formed.
- 150 million—Birds took flight, and earth broke into song.
- 120 million—Flowers covered the earth with seeds, food, color, and scents.
- 115 million—The first placental mammals evolved, and the earth entered maternal nurturing.
- 67 million—A cataclysmic crisis occurred, and dinosaurs disappeared.
- 40 million—The evolution of mammals, such as whales and elephants, was completed.
- 3 million—Last of the Ice Age began.
- 2.6 million—Earliest humanoid types developed, and the earth awoke into consciousness. Stone tools and hunting began.

"I will behold the work of your hands."
—Psalm 8

We Are What We Eat

When I was asked to give a talk on ecology at the nearby university not long ago, I shocked the students by saying that when I was petting my cat that morning, I suddenly realized that his body, teeth, claws, fur, and inner organs were all once dry cat food.

It's true. I got him as a kitten, when his body was only the size that his head is now. I had fed him for a year, and what had gone into his body (including a few birds and lizards) has been converted into what now exists as a mature cat. I guess I was just as amazed as they were when I said it.

Healthy food is converted into a healthy body. Unhealthy food is converted into an unhealthy body. It's that simple because we are, in fact, what we eat.

I raise organic food on the farm here, devoid of chemicals and pesticides, because I don't want our community to digest what is unhealthy. Unfortunately, what we purchase in stores is a mystery to us. We don't really know what that food contains, and I notice lots of hospitals going up here and there. Chickens to be sold in large numbers are now kept in cages and fed antibiotic-laced soy and corn, rather than be allowed to roam the grounds, eating insects and grasses, and they are now higher in fat than in protein for our consumption.

What's the solution? If you have land, how about growing your own vegetables and raising a few chickens for meat and eggs? Stay healthy.

Cypress Trees

A familiar scene on Louisiana postcards is that of a cypress swamp. The Spanish moss, alligators, heron, raccoons, and sometimes a houseboat always add to the scene, of course.

While marshes have high grass, swamps have trees—the majority of them cypress—that are very content to live in water. Soggy soil offers little support for trees, so species that grow in swamps have developed various adaptations to keep from falling over. One is a trunk with a swollen base, which enables such trees as the cypress to sit as solidly as tenpins, even though they grow in deep water. The woody knees protruding above the water are not supporting structures, but breathing devices that supply the underwater roots with oxygen.

Our lone cypress sits on the edge of the lake, surrounded by several knees. I once tried to saw one off in order to carve a figure, but it was too hard for me to do since I was leaning over the water, trying to balance myself.

I've seen so many lovely lamp bases and other objects in souvenir shops made from cypress knees that I'm determined to someday get in one of our canoes and try again to saw one.

Pickling Processes

When I first started making pickles from our organic garden, I thought the favorite would be the dill but discovered the bread 'n butters won out. I sold a young man two jars of them not long ago, and a few minutes later, he presented me with the empty jars, in case I wanted them back. I explained to him that they were normally eaten on sandwiches.

I was reading up on the process of pickle-making in other countries, and in India it's not cucumber that's used, but a large variety of fruits and vegetables, marinated in oil and spices.

In Japan, vegetables are preserved in soy sauce, vinegar, and rice bran, and are placed in a "pickle press" in which heavy weights are placed on the marinating vegetables for some time.

In our country, commercially produced pickles (from cucumbers, of course) contain preservatives like citric acid and sodium benzoate; however, you won't find any of those elements in what has been grown in our garden. No, sir: only vinegar, sugar, and spices.

Lizards Everywhere

It seems that almost every time I reach for a hose to start watering one of our many gardens, there's a lizard sitting on top of it. During this warm weather they're just about everywhere catching insects, but why always on the hoses? Maybe they're hoping to get to the water inside somehow.

Anyway, we would have a lot more chewed-up plants out there if it weren't for our lizards gulping down those insects. I love to watch the lizards preparing to pounce after some very slow movements toward their prey. Their tails are like rudders, helping them rapidly change direction, but it can be to a lizard's advantage to lose its tail. When a predator grabs it, the tail breaks off, and the lizard scampers to safety and grows a replacement within a month or two.

It's fascinating to watch a green lizard change to brown when switching to an object of that color. They are experts at camouflage.

On a few small Indonesian islands are found Komodo dragons, the world's largest lizards. They are twelve feet in length and resemble a combination dinosaur/dragon.

I'll bet there aren't a whole lot of insects on those islands.

My Little Ernie

Ernie, my little female cat, is remarkable. One day she got her leg injured and was limping, so I put her on the floor of the car and drove about four miles to the vet. When I opened the door to pick her up, she, who is usually very gentle, flew into the woods behind the office. We all searched until we felt it was hopeless. I felt I would never see her again.

Of course, I cried on the way home, thinking someone would find and mistreat her, or that she would get hit by a car, and I began thinking of what a joy she had been and how I would miss her. I prayed to St. Francis to take care of her and bring her back to me, and when I opened my front door about an hour later, who was standing there, looking up at me, soaking wet, but my little Ernie!

My cat had never seen any landmarks between her home and the veterinarian's office because she was on the floor of the car the times I had taken her there; however, she had walked three miles down the highway in the rain, and after passing about ten streets, she knew at which one to finally turn, and she continued on another mile to my front porch.

I headed to the store the very next day and bought a statue of St. Francis, which now stands in my little flower garden. I thank him often for guiding my little one safely home.

Moss That's Not Really Moss

I have always admired the typically southern Spanish moss that graces many of the trees in our area, although I've noticed that, unfortunately, none of it seems to have reached Rosaryville yet.

It is not scientifically classified as moss but as an air plant, which propagates by seed and fragments that blow in the wind and stick to trees, and are carried by birds as nesting material. It absorbs its nutrients and water from trees, air, and rainfall, and although it rarely kills trees, it lowers their growth rate by reducing the amount of light to their leaves.

The plant seems to prefer growing on live oaks, cypress, and crepe myrtles because these particular trees possess a high rate of nutrients they need. The plant is found in the southeast area of our country and also grows as far south as Argentina, where the weather is warm and humid.

Various purposes for which the moss has been used are building insulation, mulch, packing material, mattress stuffing, arts and crafts, flower gardens, and even stuffing for voodoo dolls.

I can't imagine looking at a scene of a Southern plantation without that graceful Spanish moss cascading from the branches of live oaks. I think I'll find some nearby and start draping it on our trees and see what happens.

Nocturnal Neighbors in Our Woods

There used to be lots of bunnies hopping around here—a pleasant sight if you don't have a garden.

Now, we don't see any. Why? Coyotes probably took care of them, poor little things.

Those coyotes prowl the woods at night searching for small animals. I worry about my cats, as the coyotes don't hesitate to eat them if they get too close.

Coyotes, also called jackals and prairie wolves, are found all the way from Panama to Alaska, and there are nineteen recognized species. They grow to about three feet in length and two feet in height, with a tail of about fifteen inches. The largest coyote on record was five feet tall.

A couple of us saw one during the day not long ago, and we didn't know what it was because it didn't have the dimensions of a normal-sized dog. It was a little scary.

In the movies, coyotes always lift their heads and howl. Not in these woods, thank goodness. All we hear are crickets and frogs.

Rain Sends Underground Creatures Up

Because of all of the rain lately, lots of little creatures have surfaced from down below to provide tasty meals in the grass for our feathered friends. Down the road from us there are fields with lots of cows—and lots of white birds that hang around the cows and sit on top of them, searching for food in the form of fleas or some such insects, I suppose. But it seems most of them lately have left the cows out in the pasture to swoop down on our grounds to have a feast on whatever little creatures are floating up out of their homes. Those white heads are bobbing up and down constantly. If they stayed still, they'd look like large patches of snow on the green grass.

I asked a nearby farmer what kind of birds they were, with their curved beaks and short legs and necks, and he replied, "Cow birds." I thanked him kindly and later found out they're called cattle egrets—a little more sophisticated name, I'd say.

One of Our Many Blessings

How wonderful to have a friend who owns a mushroom farm. Every now and then, she blesses us with a couple of boxes of those delicacies, much of which I sauté and freeze for future use in cooking so as not to lose any.

Mushrooms are the best known of the more than 75,000 species of plants classified as fungi; their tiny reproductive units are called spores, which are released by the billions as dust that can travel with the wind for thousands of miles.

When landing in damp places, mushrooms can grow and develop overnight, and they may take on an endless array of forms and colors. The nutritional analysis of mushrooms (those that are not poisonous, that is) reads as a dream to those who are really health minded.

When we barbecue on special days, I bite down on my delicious grilled portabella burger on a bun with all the dressings, aware of the nutrients, minimal calories, lack of fat, and cholesterol, and I say, "Eat your heart out, McDonald's."

Gold in the Pond

When the first hint of spring was in the air, I got the urge to clean the large fishpond out by the grotto. I hadn't seen the goldfish during the cold weather because in the winter they hardly eat and try to stay out of sight. Suddenly, on that first warm day, there they were, happily swimming around, still the same small size as when I had bought them a couple of months earlier.

The goldfish are not too pretty now because it takes a while for them to turn that golden color we admire. (I don't want them to know I chose them instead of the big, pretty ones because they were only ten for a dollar.) I read that some have been known to live as long as forty years, and some attain the length of two feet, weighing as much as ten pounds. Well, hopefully mine won't do that.

Goldfish don't really care a lot about dieting, so they shouldn't be fed more than they can eat in about three minutes. And speaking of eating, after the babies are born, if they are not separated from the adults, the poor little things can become a hearty meal.

I was happy to read that the United Kingdom and the city of Rome—and maybe other places—have banned the sale of those small goldfish bowls in pet shops because confining them to such small spaces is cruel. I totally agree.

Those Welcome Raindrops

I guess it's especially people like me, who care for large gardens, who are always hoping to see a dark cloud in the sky. Moisture rises from bodies of water, trees, and plants and condenses into drops as clouds, and when the clouds become heavy with dust particles, the moisture returns to earth as rain, as we all know.

I've always imagined raindrops as teardrop shaped, but the small and medium drops are perfectly round; and the large ones look like parachutes. At least, that's what I read.

Although Seattle has an average of 201 cloudy days per year, Mobile, Alabama, is the wettest city in the country, having an average of 67 inches of rain annually. I'll bet the farmers there have the biggest harvests around, while the rest of us are dragging out those hoses most of the summer.

Scraps for Beggars

While on the porch a few evenings ago, a furry little masked creature peeped through the railing and looked up at me as if to say, "Haven't you forgotten something?"

Living at a retreat center where food gets scraped into a container after meals by a number of retreatants, I can see no sense in allowing leftovers to be simply thrown away. After collecting those scraps, I take them to the edge of the woods in the evening, where I know they will be deeply appreciated by our raccoons who live in there and who are shyly waiting for their supper. Only after I have left do they come out to eat. My little friend who lets me know when I've forgotten them from time to time isn't quite so shy.

Raccoons are not destructive like the armadillos who turn up my garden every night, so I don't mind them wandering around after dark, foraging for more food than I've given them. However, at night I do have to hide the fish food I carry in the golf cart; if not, I'll find the empty jar several yards from the cart the next morning. Those five little fingers, including a thumb, are capable of unscrewing caps.

These little creatures might be bothersome at times, but with their little masks and striped tails they're awfully cute.

Respecting Wildlife

When I return home after dark, I turn on my bright lights so I can see the eyes of deer shining like little lights in our woods. They're very shy and don't ever come out during the day, unfortunately. They're such beautiful animals. I would love to watch them grazing on our grounds here and there.

Some friends visiting from the Missouri/Illinois area spoke of the number of deer they had seen lying dead on the sides of the roads. The opening of the hunting season would explain it, as so much of their natural habitats are being taken from them with the leveling of numerous forests. There aren't many places for them to run for safety except, very often, toward the highways. What a tragedy.

I certainly approve of deer being hunted for food, as they would continue to increase in number to a point of starvation, but I hope and pray that hunters are sensitive enough to make sure they don't suffer unnecessarily before dying. These are God's creatures who didn't ask to be born. They feel pain as we do and don't deserve to be treated as inanimate objects.

Short-Lived Cicadas

If any insect knows anything about resurrection, it's the cicada.

During their maturing stage, many cicadas remain underground for as long as seventeen years before emerging to view the trees and sky that have been hidden from view all that time.

When a brood does emerge, they can number in the thousands. They immediately climb up trees and fences and shed their skins. As children, we used to love to collect those prickly little shells.

After molting, the adult flying cicada lives only about four to six weeks, and you can hear the males' mating songs in the trees from early morning until nightfall. It's such a pleasant experience for me to sit outside in the evening, immersed in their symphony as the sun sets behind our woods.

Between five and ten days after mating, the female cuts slits in deciduous trees, which shed leaves annually, and she lays her eggs. She can deposit up to six hundred of them here and there, and when they hatch, the tiny nymphs fall to the ground and burrow into the soil, feasting on underground roots until they finally emerge years later.

There are actually recipes on how to cook the mature, winged cicadas. The hard part would be catching them. I really think I'd rather listen to them than eat them.

Our Golden Honey

This afternoon, when I reached for the jar of honey to put in my hot tea, that same sensation of awe overcame me as I thought of the source and incredible process that produces this golden treasure.

I often drive out of my way in the golf cart to observe the honeybees around the hive behind the barn, and I try to imagine the queen bee laying thousands of eggs in there, while depending on all the others to collect the nectar, take care of the young, and produce the honey.

It's always such an exciting event to collect that sweet, golden substance, but the beekeeping industry has been plagued lately by parasitic mites and the mysterious phenomenon known as colony collapse. This simply means that the bees abandon their hives and don't return. It happened to us here on our grounds. The hives were suddenly empty, after producing many pounds of delicious honey. It was heartbreaking.

I read that we can do something positive in our gardens to make a difference. Yellow, purple, and blue flowers are honeybee magnets. They also prefer wild blooms to overbred inventions with lots of petals and little pollen.

I've planted yellow and purple lantanas and blue plumbagos in our Peace Garden, and I hope this brings some of our precious friends back.

The Necessity of Awareness

While sitting out on one of those beautiful days, I noticed a lizard resting peacefully on a branch.

I was fascinated by the inward and outward movement of its belly as it breathed, and I thought of how intricate and amazing its tiny respiratory system was. Then I thought of its digestive, muscular, reproductive, and nervous systems. I went on to think of those systems of the very smallest of animals and insects, and it was all mind-boggling.

I don't allow myself to kill any of these little creatures unless it's absolutely necessary. At times there are a few exceptions, but I can't help but reverence those incredible creations of God living out their short lives, following their instincts in the realm of nature surrounding us.

Those Little Birds That Hum

What a delightful surprise to see my first hummingbird of the season on our grounds yesterday morning, hovering over the spot where I hung the sugar water for the birds last summer. How on earth did it remember that spot, after having migrated far from here for several months?

What fascinating little creatures! Beating those little wings about seventy-five times per second, causing a humming sound, gave them their name. They can fly right, left, up, down, backward, and even upside down, and they can hover in a figure-eight pattern. They use their feet only to perch— not to hop or walk as do other birds. Their heart beats 1,260 times per minute; they weigh less than an ounce but proportionately have the largest brain of all birds—more than 4 percent of their body weight.

Hummingbirds are very territorial, chasing each other away from the food and even chasing larger birds, such as hawks. Courageous little things.

Spring and Maple Syrup Time

As young Sisters we were always served cane syrup and peanut butter for snacks, as there were many sugarcane fields in Louisiana, including at the Benedictine monastery nearby, and the syrup was abundant. Maple syrup was found on our store shelves but always was very expensive. Now I know why.

In the past, openings were bored in the maple trees up north and tubes inserted, through which the sap leaked into buckets. These were collected by horse-drawn sleds throughout the day and taken to the sugar house for processing.

While I was in Quebec not long ago, friends took me to view the modern system for collecting sap. The tube traveled through the snow-covered woods, parallel to the ground, to its destination—the boiling pot in the sugar house. It wasn't as picturesque a scene as in the past, but the method certainly was less laborious.

Each tree produces about three buckets of sap a day, and it takes forty gallons of it to produce only one gallon of syrup. This explains why maple syrup is so expensive. Down here in the South, we'll just keep pouring our own delicious cane syrup on our pancakes.

A Louisiana Treasure

L ately I've been noticing lots of crayfish holes with the dirt from down below piled high around the top, crafted very artistically. As often as I have seen these, I have yet to see the process in action. The little mudbugs must be awfully busy at night when no one is around.

These small, delicious creatures are eaten all around the world, with Louisiana producing as much as 90 percent of them; its average annual harvest is approximately 55,000 tons.

Crayfish boils are especially popular in southern Louisiana. The tail, of course, is the part that is eaten, but since much of the seasoning and flavor collect in the fat of the head, a popular local saying is, "Suck the head; pinch the tail."

Fossils of these little crustaceans tell us they have been around for about 115 million years, and it is jokingly said that they all start up north as lobsters, and by the time they reach the South they are worn-out and smaller.

What could be more tempting than a long table of steaming crayfish, corn on the cob, and potatoes, all cooked in red pepper, garlic, and other tantalizing spices, eaten out under the trees on a spring day?

The Miracle of Capistrano

S everal years ago, while attending a conference in Los Angeles, a friend and I slipped out early one morning to visit the famous Mission of San Juan Capistrano nearby. We were interested not only in its history, beauty, and peace, but we also wanted to be able to say we had toured the church and grounds where a miraculous phenomenon occurs annually.

Since 1776, flocks of swallows have returned to the mission every March 19 after their period of migration, and numerous tourists are on hand to witness this remarkable occurrence.

So, every year on the feast of St. Joseph, the swallows announce to the Californians that spring has arrived, and they settle again at their beloved mission for the summer months.

Maybe I should contact the Franciscans there to discover what it might take to begin such a phenomenon here.

Our Goldfish Have New Neighbors

Our goldfish, who have been enjoying having the little pond near the grotto all to themselves, suddenly find themselves sharing it with about one thousand tadpoles. It's that time of year when the female frogs have to search out a body of water in which to lay their eggs, and boy, do they ever lay some eggs!

Each year in May, I've found long, clear strips (like movie film) dotted with tiny black eggs that go on forever, wrapped around the water plants and whatever else is in the pond. If you find the strips in time, they can be pulled out before they dissolve, allowing the eggs to go off in every direction and quickly become tadpoles. Within a few weeks, they undergo a remarkable transformation to land-dwelling frogs, as legs are formed and the tail disappears.

Frogs make up the largest, most familiar group of amphibians. Under water, tadpoles first breathe with gills, which gradually are replaced by lungs for life out of water.

I've noticed lately that the number of tadpoles out there has decreased somewhat. It might have something to do with the goldfish gaining a little weight.

The Joy of Snakes

When spring arrived, I was sitting near our lake reading, and out of the corner of my eye I saw some movement in the water right near the shore. I suddenly realized that it was snake season, and sure enough, it was a small water moccasin writhing through the tall grasses with determination. Then there was another, and another—all the same size.

Obviously, they were from the same mother who must have been nearby, which made me a little nervous since they are poisonous. Of course, the little ones weren't interested in me; they were just interested in exploring this world into which they had just arrived.

It is during this time of year that I find dried skins here and there that older snakes have shed when molting. The skin is a tissuelike impression of the body, scales and all. Right before it molts, the snake is uncomfortable and more aggressive; also, its eyes cloud over, and it goes into hiding until they clear. When they emerge, they brush against rough surfaces to pull the old skin away.

I've seen king snakes, garter snakes, and others around that are not poisonous, but I always make sure to drag my feet slowly when in high grass just in case one of those cottonmouths, copperheads, or moccasins is around.

I read that the king cobra of Asia can reach a length of eighteen feet and has enough venom to kill twenty people or more. Oh, boy.

The Splendor of Azaleas

Every day I'm noticing more and more color appearing on the many azalea bushes on our grounds after having been dormant for a year. What a wonderful performance of Mother Nature to usher in this season each year.

Azalea bushes have so many stems that during the flowering season they are a solid mass of pink, white, or purple, blooming all at once. Because of the short duration of the flower's yearly splendor, admirers flock to public gardens, display indoor bouquets and take photos to remember the spectacle.

Plant enthusiasts have nurtured azaleas for hundreds of years, and there are now more than ten thousand varieties that have been propagated by cuttings. Many places such as Bellengrath Gardens in Mobile, Alabama, draw thousands to celebrate the spectacle of blooms, and the azalea trail in Tyler, Texas, is a whopping eight miles long.

Those camellias and azaleas that array our grounds only once a year are preserved on note cards printed for our gift shop, as well as, of course, in my own photo albums.

Stocking Stuffing

On a couple of those beautiful days this week, I sat out under the trees near the stable and did my annual "stuffing" project.

Yes, it's time again to think of warding off the deer in our woods from roaming during the night through my large vegetable garden, which should start producing in a few weeks.

From the local hair salons I pick up large boxes of hair, and in old stockings I've collected from friends I stuff the hair to hang all around the fence enclosing my garden.

You see, the eyesight of a deer isn't too great, but its sense of smell is exceptional. When they get a whiff of humans in the dark they naturally think some of them are out there in hiding. The scent lasts for several months, and I have yet to find any traces of deer near my crops during that time.

I stopped planting watermelons because of the rats drilling holes in them and cleaning out the insides, but now that I have three cats I can feel a little safer. Oh, the trials of a farmer.

Those Red Swamp Maples

Springtime has definitely arrived. While driving to New Orleans along Owl Bayou a few days ago, I witnessed a continuous panorama of red maples mingled with the light greens of various other trees in the marshes.

To add to the beauty, there was a flock of white heron stretching out for quite a long distance over the water against that colorful background. That's when I jumped out of the car with my camera.

Most of the trees on our grounds are evergreens, but the maples are the ones that treat us to a show of brilliant, deep scarlet leaves in the fall. They can reach a height of fifty feet, can live as long as 150 years, and can be used on a small scale for maple syrup.

Syrup or no syrup, they grow quickly, add oxygen to the air, and are beautiful to behold. Little more can you ask from a tree.

St. Joseph Altars

S ometimes, something that appears to be a disaster may turn out to be a blessing. Today there would be no such tradition among Italians as the St. Joseph Altars, so numerous in this area, had it not been for serious crop failures in Sicily in the nineteenth century.

The poor farmers turned to St. Joseph to intercede for them in their plight, promising to build altars on his feast day each March 19 on which food from their farms would be placed to be given to the poor. With answered prayers and bountiful harvests, they kept their promise and continue to do so today in this country.

In our Italian communities in this area, altars are constructed every March and filled with statues, candles, flowers, and a variety of foods. They are viewed by hundreds to honor their special saint on his feast.

Today's altars certainly are more elaborate than those of the poor farmers in Italy, but the simple faith and sincerity of those Italian ancestors remain, and out of continued gratitude, the poor are still being fed.

A Heritage Celebrated

Yes, the Italians in this area really have something to celebrate each spring. The Italian Festival takes place in a nearby town on the last weekend of April, when the strawberry season is at its peak, and the Italians recall their ancestors arriving several generations ago and developing the strawberry farms so numerous in this area of southeast Louisiana.

These little plants derived their name in the early days from the straw that was used as their mulch. Adults who grew up here recall how, when they were children, the straw was dumped along the rows on top of the small plants, and how they had to follow and remove the straw from their tops and spread it around them.

When we were children in the New Orleans, my father used to add a few strawberry plants to his vegetable garden in order to show us how they grew. Of course, being city kids, all we did was look at them and eat them.

Here in Rosaryville we grew strawberries for many years. The young Sisters would pick and pack them in the little shed out by the field and sell them in town. We ate the berries with every meal during the spring and early summer, and a couple of us at a time spent at least an hour every afternoon— one cranking the handle of that old machine while another sat on top to hold it down—making our supper dessert of, you guessed it, strawberry ice cream.

A Protective Father

For the past week there has been a mockingbird flying from tree to roof, to car, to driveway, and back to tree, squawking every couple of seconds. He's very upset because obviously he doesn't trust three cats roaming around his nest, where the mother bird is sitting on eggs.

My cats are totally ignoring him and continuing to go about their business of exploring, sleeping, and eating. I only wish I could ignore the racket out there.

Yesterday, when I put the cat food on the porch and one cat was headed to eat, the bird actually flew down to the ground, squawking and hopping behind him for a short distance. It was quite a sight, and finally a period of humor.

The mother bird has to remain on those eggs, giving them eighty degrees of heat from her body and turning them to keep them evenly heated throughout the day. Her feathers may be a hindrance at this time because they block the transfer of body heat, and most species molt some belly feathers at incubation time.

When hatching time arrives, the chick revolves in the shell, chipping a circular groove all the way around. This may take a few hours or several days. After a long rest, it gives a powerful heave with its neck, the end of the shell falls off, and the bedraggled bird emerges.

I suppose the bedraggled father will finally give his squawking a rest when this happens: soon, hopefully.

Sure Sign of Spring

I see some busy little birds around here lately, flying with pieces of paper, twigs, pine needles, and other little items hanging from their bills and heading for the construction site of their new nests. (My friend had one bird land on her head as she sat still reading and chose a few strands of hair that would do nicely.)

I read that in most species the female does all or most of the nest construction, though the male often helps. However, males of certain species, such as weaver birds, do all of the building, which is part of their courtship endeavors; the female scouts around to find the nest built of the highest quality before jumping in it and proclaiming, "I'm yours!"

Hummingbirds have the smallest nests—tiny cups that can be less than one inch across and about one inch high. At the other extreme, some nests built by the Dusky Scrubfowl measure more than thirty-four feet in diameter and stand nearly fifteen feet tall. I hope there are none of those around here.

Spring Awakenings

There I was yesterday, sitting out in my lawn chair and thinking of my day ahead: Gather more manure across the road, collect more decayed oak leaves in the woods, buy the nutrients for the soil that the agricultural center suggested, plant that little pepper bush my friend gave me, buy more plants to replace those that died in the hard frost, etc. And then it happened. A big raindrop hit my head.

So much for the day's plans, I thought. But a little later, after a nice shower, I returned outdoors to find a gorgeous blue sky and leaves and grass sparkling like diamonds.

Speaking of diamonds, when I finished my chores for the day, I looked up to the west at twilight and saw the beautiful planet Venus. Right above it was the moon half full, in anticipation of Holy Week, when it will shine in its full glory.

Many farmers plant during that week. This, they believe, will result in an abundant harvest. That's one thing I'll be doing, too, besides basking in the new life all around me.

Honey of a Creature

When I was with my family in New Orleans for Mardi Gras, I was surprised to see a lone honeybee hovering over the food we had sitting out most of the day during the parades. I asked him what he was doing on St. Charles Avenue, maybe miles from his beehive, and later I learned honeybees can fly as far as three and a half miles while searching for nectar.

I suppose there must be some beehives in those live oaks lining the avenue, and I know bees even set up hives in walls of houses; however, the unfortunate situation today is that our honeybees are rapidly decreasing in number due, in many cases, to the type of pesticides being used.

Having observed the bees here in our gardens, it's hard to believe that it is possible to have fifty thousand of them in one colony, producing about two and a half pounds of honey a day while hidden within the darkness of their hive.

As the bee alights on the petal of a flower, its weight causes a stamen to swing down, and the bee is dusted with pollen to be carried to the next flower. It is estimated that more than one quarter of the human diet is derived from plants pollinated by those little creatures, who beat their wings about 180 times per second during flight.

They seem to be as busy as can be in the big cities as well as in the country.

Homeless Creatures

With the arrival of the hurricane season down here, my mind has been very much with the homeless, as my being without a home is something I can't even imagine. Of course, storms don't only affect humans, but animals also.

During our last hurricane, a small tornado swept through our grounds, uprooting about a dozen large trees in its path. The next day, it almost broke my heart to see a bird flying into one of the fallen trees, probably searching for the nest it had painstakingly built, and in it, the young it had been protecting.

Also, I haven't seen the five raccoons I've been feeding every evening, or the hummingbirds that were frequenting my feeder. Are they temporarily homeless, also? How blessed are those of us who have never experienced this misfortune.

Lack of Awareness

These days, everywhere I walk there are acorns and pine seeds scattered all over the grounds, being ignored, stepped on, and raked up, often with the attitude, "What a mess."

That "mess" consists of amazing, life-bearing sources of mighty oaks and majestic pines that will never reach their potential. Being aware of the nature of these small miracles lying on the ground, I try to avoid as many as possible in my path.

This morning, that same sense of awe came over me as I held an egg in my hand and realized it had within it the potential of a new life. My mind then switched to the thought of the hen that had laid it, and I couldn't help thinking of the cruelty experienced by these little creatures in many factories.

Being jammed into crowded cages, unable to spread their wings, scratch the soil, enjoy dust baths, or search for insects, chickens often end up fighting, so they are debeaked, which makes it painful for them to eat. Also, in order to force molting for them to produce more eggs, they are deprived of food and water for periods of time.

We can live on the surface, or we can live on a higher plane, being sensitive to, and respecting, all forms of life surrounding us.

Our Children and Nature

It's spring, and I can't imagine deliberately closing myself inside to sit in front of a computer or TV instead of basking in the unfolding of nature's new life outside all around us.

My childhood was filled with, among other things, skating, playing hopscotch, jumping rope, climbing trees, playing with pets, and planting to watch things grow. Indoors was for school, studying, eating, and sleeping.

I remember reading a book in which the author reveals a direct connection between the absence of nature in the lives of today's youth and its negative health and societal impacts, notably attention disorders, depression, and obesity.

When I was running our summer camp out here, I recall the nurse next to me collecting a huge amount of medications from the parents for the children to take daily. I couldn't believe my eyes and ears. All I can remember our taking as children was cod liver oil with orange juice every morning, and I don't recall our getting sick except for the common measles and mumps that most children got.

I pray that parents will become aware of the necessity of their children's healthy involvement with God's handiwork outdoors rather than with electronics, the work of human hands.

Nature's Medicine

While enjoying an annual Easter camping trip with my family in Gulf Shores, Alabama, I noticed very few children on the campground and thought of how sad that was.

I read an article not long ago about our children needing to be saved from "nature deficit disorder." The author states that many kids of the digital age have become increasingly alienated from nature and are paying a price, not only in their physical condition but also in their mental and spiritual health.

Hopefully, we soon will be seeing more children leave behind their TVs, cell phones, and computers for the seashore and woods. Being surrounded by God's handiwork has a dynamic effect on our well-being regardless of age; it can, in fact, add years to our lives.

As a child, we thought indoors was only for eating, sleeping, and school. I still grab every minute I can to be outdoors surrounded by God's handiwork.

Menacing Mosquitoes

The number of mosquitoes out here in Rosaryville is unbelievable. I guess with all the rain this spring it was bound to happen. The female lays her eggs in standing water, so we're careful to go around the buildings to empty containers, since the liquid can become their nurseries these days.

The adult male mosquito can feed just on nectar and plant juice and lives for about a week, but the female, who can live for a month, needs "blood meals" before producing eggs. During these blood feedings, the females inject their sources with saliva, which serves as an anticoagulant, or blood thinner (the cause of that awful itching); without it, her proboscis would quickly become clogged.

There are about 3,500 species of mosquitoes throughout the world, and they are known to transmit disease to more than 700 million people annually, causing the death of at least 2 million.

Sorry, God; I can easily praise you for most of your creations, but I find it a little difficult to be thankful for these little creatures as I spray myself with repellant while working on the grounds.

A Fairyland of Pear Blossoms

While standing in a grove of pear trees at the beginning of March, I actually do feel that I have been plucked up and placed in a far-off fairyland while under those canopies of white blossoms.

The majority of these trees, I'm told, are Bradford pears, which grow small fruit eaten by birds when ripe. Besides the beauty they display in the spring, they are a sight to behold in the fall, when their leaves turn fiery red.

When I was growing up in New Orleans, we would climb the "cooking pear" tree in our yard with our little knives, sit on the branches, and peel and eat those delicious hard pears to our hearts' content. My grandmother would cook and preserve many of them, also. We would have to get the soft "eating pears" from the grocery store.

Pear trees go way back as far as prehistoric times, and about three thousand known varieties grow worldwide, China being their top producer. In the U.S., however, only ten heirloom varieties are recognized and sold.

Besides being a delight to our taste buds, pears are a valuable source of treating arthritis and lowering high blood pressure and cholesterol.

By the way, to get them to ripen quickly, put them in a bowl next to some bananas.

Motherhood and Mother Nature

Each year countries set aside a special day to honor mothers—those who have brought new life into the world. Life, growth, maturity, and death—parts of the life cycle of nature—are always within our sight and reach.

Have you ever held a seed in your hand and contemplated its potential? When planted under proper conditions, life unfolds silently in darkness, enters into light, grows until it has reached its potential, and then makes possible new life from its own existence.

A seed consists of an embryo, a supplier of nutrients for the embryo, and a coat that protects it. Does all that sound familiar? Mother Nature is aptly named. When we think of how we all began, and what was involved in our arriving in this world, we really need to celebrate motherhood more than once a year.

We are all miracles of nature who began as seeds. This leads me to the unbelievable story of when, in 2005, excavations of the palace of Herod the Great in Israel were under way, a 2,000-year-old seed was discovered, planted, and actually germinated!

Those Happy Blackbirds

Here they come, every morning: large swarms of blackbirds diving in unison on certain areas of our grounds, and then later swooping into a tree in another wave of black.

It's when they're up on the branches that they begin their loud, ear-splitting music—or just plain racket. Whatever it is, it sounds happy.

These little birds are found just about everywhere in the world. The males are solid black with a yellow eye ring and bill, and the females and juveniles have brown plumage and bills.

It seems they received their name around the eighteenth century in the British Isles. There, the word "bird" was used for smaller birds, and the word "fowl" for larger birds, and since small, black birds were so common, they were simply named "blackbirds."

I remember from childhood the words in the English nursery rhyme, "Four and twenty blackbirds baked in a pie. When the pie was opened, the birds began to sing..." Strange.

It's interesting that the males sing a rich, melodious song, but only between March and June; during the other months, they just call and squawk. They also can imitate other birds, like the mockingbird does.

I must admit that I really enjoy the show and the joyful sounds every morning these spring days as I sit on my porch with my coffee.

Swamp Friends

One of the latest attractions out here on many of these warm days is the sight of an alligator floating in the middle of our lake, lazily soaking up the sun. That's fine as long as he stays out there. Some of the creatures that wander out of our swamp may be only six feet long but can grow to about fifteen feet.

Alligators and crocodiles are found only in the southeastern part of our country, and although most reptiles never utter a sound, these let out a loud roar during mating season. (I hope I never hear that out here—especially at night.)

The female is an extraordinary parent in that, unlike other reptiles, after laying between twenty and sixty eggs in a hole she has dug and covered with vegetation, she remains with them for ten weeks, turning them to maintain an even temperature until they hatch.

The alligator's close relative, the slender-snouted crocodile, lives in southern Florida and grows to a larger size.

A zookeeper once told me that alligators can run fast, but they tire out after about twenty-five feet. That's something to remember when you're being chased.

Butterflies Enhance Our Gardens

Those beautiful, multi-colored monarch butterflies have been returning to our southern shores all this month, so I've gotten myself to the nursery to purchase milkweed and lantana plants to attract them to our large garden near the chapel.

In the late summer, every monarch butterfly in North America heads south to Mexico—a trip that can take six weeks. Millions of them perch on pine trees there until March and then fly back to us to lay their eggs.

As a teacher, I once carried around a chrysalis in school for days, awaiting the emergence of the full-grown butterfly; when the event started happening, my classroom was filled with breathless students witnessing the miracle.

Butterflies will afford us the privilege of beautifying our grounds until they begin their endless cycle all over again in the fall. Until then, I'll have to distract my cats, who can jump almost five feet straight up to nab one.

Taking Turns at the Feeder

I always make sure to keep the birdbath and feeder filled during these hot months because I love to witness the show of splashing and eating that results, especially early in the morning.

The feeder I had purchased was inexpensive. I hadn't noticed it had nothing on which the birds could perch while eating, so I nailed four Popsicle sticks in the forms of two crosses to protrude from the bottom on two sides.

This morning as I watched, I saw that some birds were waiting their turn, and some even were fighting to get to stand on the feeder to eat. Now I know that I have to take it in and nail two more landing places for them.

Whatever trouble it takes—the food, the water, the perches—it's all worth it to observe God's little creatures being satisfied.

It's Nice to Be Serenaded

This morning while weeding in our enclosed Peace Garden, I decided to take a break for a while, and what an enjoyable break it was.

As soon as I sat in the rocker on the porch, a mockingbird alighted on the cross high up on the steeple and began singing. It's amazing that they are capable of imitating so many other birds. I believe that during the time I sat there he almost completed his entire repertoire.

Not only was he serenading me; he kept flying straight up and then back down on his perch, over and over again. He was doing a dance to accompany his singing, seeing that he had a captive audience, I suppose.

When I went outside the building to weed another garden—I don't know whether or not it was my same friend—a mockingbird alighted on a limb right above me, and the music continued.

That was just about the most enjoyable weeding session I've ever had.

A Small Price to Pay

I wonder why the gnats in the morning and mosquitoes in the evening feel I need company when I'm out in the field hoeing my garden. A horsefly usually comes around also to see what I'm doing and how much it can annoy me.

And then there are the wild turkeys roaming around, enjoying my fresh little seedlings just coming up. Of all our seventeen hundred acres where they could find food, they instead head for my garden.

About those gnats—I read it's the males who assemble together in swarms while searching for mates; as far as the mosquitoes, it's the females that sting us.

Despite all of this, it's a gift to be living in the country surrounded by so much beauty, especially this time of year. I guess those annoying pests, who were here first, are a small price to pay.

The Blessings of Rain

Our birds here in Rosaryville certainly loved all of that rain lately. After those downpours, large swarms would appear and light on our grounds to peck away at the little creatures surfacing from their flooded homes. The frogs, crickets, and ducks also enjoyed it—but not as much as I did.

I thought of the terrible drought we experienced last summer, and whenever I'd hear "this nasty weather," "terrible outside," or "when will it ever end?" I'd silently say, "Thank you, God. Don't pay any attention to them."

The awareness of all the thirsty roots of our trees and large bushes being sufficiently soaked, and of our wells being replenished, was enough for me to accept the dealings with umbrellas, slow traffic, and wet shoes. Also, I very often think of the unnerving fact that only 1 percent of the flowing water on our planet is fresh and drinkable, and another 1 percent is stored in glaciers, which are melting.

Our attitudes are always empowered by our knowledge.

New Life in the Garden

Once spring had arrived this year, I checked several nurseries for vincas, or periwinkles, but I was told that because of the heavy freeze last winter they were slow in arriving.

At the center, a couple of weeks after digging up all my dead vincas, I suddenly discovered lots of tiny seedlings where the mother plants had been, and I realized that before they froze they had dropped their seeds all around the area.

I bought dozens of little peat pots and transplanted the vincas to await their growth of a few inches. They are such hardy and colorful plants; they grow well in the sun as well as shade, and they have bunches of flowers on each plant.

Throughout the entire summer my garden is alive with blue plumbagos, gold lantanas, pink begonias, and multi-colored zinnias, roses, and vincas.

What a sight to behold.

Enchanted Corner

Last summer I spotted a small, unusual plant in the corner of our St. Francis garden. I allowed it to stay, and it became large and full, crowned with several purple, daisylike flowers. I discovered they were coneflowers, and within the lower leaves were twenty-one blooms. A bird, on its way home after eating from the feeder, must have dropped the seed there.

Another strange coincidence: This summer, without my planting it, a sunflower plant appeared right there on that same spot. It grew so tall and majestic that I decided I would plant some there every year. When I told a friend of mine about birds dropping seeds in my garden after leaving the feeder, he told me maybe that was their way of saying "thank you." What a nice thought.

Now I often sit on the porch and admire those bright yellow petals surrounding that large center filled with seeds, the sunflower following the sun throughout the day.

Several years ago, while driving along some roads in Spain to visit the home of our founder, St. Dominic, we passed miles and miles of sunflowers swaying in the breeze. What a sight to behold!

I can't wait to discover what one of our feathered friends will grace us with next summer in that enchanted corner of the garden.

When Troubles Fade Away

I dearly love rain, as all gardeners do, but after a week of downpours, it was impossible to get into the vegetable garden without mud up to my ankles, as I struggled to pull my feet up without leaving my shoes behind. I would see those perfect squash, cucumbers, and other vegetables sitting down there saying, "Pick me!" but just couldn't get to them.

Finally, after a few days of sun, it was a joy to walk on solid ground, and when I heard thunder in the distance, I did something I never do: I prayed for the rain to stay away.

Problems such as soft mud, insects, and weeds sort of fade away when I reach down to pick the gift of those beautiful vegetables and continue to say to myself, "What a miracle; I placed a tiny seed down there, left it up to God, and now this!"

The Joy of Rabbits

While buying seeds this week, I saw a cage full of small white bunnies for sale for Easter, and of course I immediately began to worry about them being neglected and treated like toys by children receiving them.

As a child, I couldn't wait to get home from school to play with my bunny, and I always made sure it had enough food and water.

The Easter Bunny had its origin in pre-Christian fertility lore, as the rabbit was the most fertile animal known and served as a symbol of new life during the spring season.

Around here, there used to be quite a few rabbits hopping in and out of the woods, and we were entertained by their playfulness; that is, before the vegetable gardens were planted. They all seem to have disappeared from the grounds — possibly because of the arrival of some coyotes in the area.

I would want the rabbits to be well fed and happy out there, but I'm not so sure how cute I would think they were if they were demolishing my carrots, lettuce, and whatever else I had in my gardens every spring and fall.

Those Little Diggers

While at a friend's house observing her garden, I noticed her lawn had little mounds of soil running several feet here and there, and I was told it was the work of moles.

I have only seen moles in pictures, and evidently we don't have any here on our grounds. We actually see our armadillos in action though, or the result of their visit the night before, when we find plants uprooted as they had searched for food.

I read that moles are rarely seen, for they spend most of their lives underground. As they tunnel in search of earthworms, insect grubs, and similar prey, moles "swim" through the soil by pushing the dirt aside with their powerfully clawed, paddlelike front feet.

Their sensitive snouts and keen sense of smell apparently are very helpful for navigating the underground darkness. The ability to detect vibrations in the soil is useful for locating prey and escaping from enemies, but their poor eyesight probably serves only to distinguish darkness from light.

While the armadillos stay above the ground, digging holes down through the soft soil in my garden, the moles living under my friend's lawn a few miles away push up the dirt every few yards. Considering how hard these little creatures of God have to work for their food, I think we'll just have to practice more patience with them.

Life-Giving Water

During the summer months I spend lots of time watering the gardens here on the grounds, while thanking God for those Benedictine monks who drilled our deep well in the 1800s. We use the well not only for our gardens but more importantly for drinking, cooking, and bathing for our numerous retreatants.

Almost a third of people in developing countries have no access to clean water. Ninety-eight percent of the water on our planet is salt water, unfit for human consumption, and as our population increases, freshwater use and wastage will continue.

More than half of the world's major rivers are being seriously depleted and polluted, and I think of families in poor countries who, very early in the morning, scrape dew from the grass for their source of water.

It's our responsibility to the rest of the world to be aware of the gift of water that is ours, and to conserve and protect it for future generations.

Fourth of July Reflections

As we pulled out the barbecue pit and displayed fireworks yesterday, our normal life of serenity gave way to that of loud celebration—a celebration of freedom.

Through the courage and perseverance of our founding fathers, our ancestors were finally able to separate themselves from British rule more than two hundred years ago on a hot summer day that was devoid of barbecued chicken and potato salad.

Freedom has long been a blessing for our nation, along with many other blessings such as those about which we sing with pride and gratefulness: "amber waves of grain and purple mountain majesties above the fruited plains."

A nation whose soil gives us bountiful crops and offers us so much beauty is one for which we must continue to raise our voices in song: "America, America, God shed His grace on thee."

Beauty of the Beach

Vacation time. I was basking in the sun on the white sands along the Gulf of Mexico last week. It was quite a switch from woods, extensive grounds of trees and gardens, and chapel bells.

We're all spoiled by the brilliant white sand beaches along our gulf coast, but this doesn't exist on all seashores. I've been to places where the sand is actually brown. What a shock that was.

It's hard to believe the fine sand on which we walk along the water's edge was once solid rock, weathered and decomposed by the elements of nature to which it had been exposed.

The most extensive deposits are seen, of course, in the desert, and much of it is used in the manufacture of bricks, concrete, pottery, and glass. An unpleasant use of sand is the manufacture of explosives, and a *very* unpleasant experience of it is biting down on some in your sandwich while picnicking on the beach.

Nature's Symphonies

I don't know if it's because of a lack of rain that the frogs and crickets these summer nights are so vocal.

When I walk outside and hear the uninterrupted, orchestrated croaking and chirpings at such a high pitch throughout the woods behind our buildings, I have to stop and soak it all in, thinking that maybe I should record it.

As I sit on the back steps to listen, my three cats, Timmy, Toby, and Ernie, quietly come up from behind and sit next to me, motionless, to share in my meditative experience.

Then at dawn, when I'm on the porch with my coffee (and cats), I am again enraptured, this time by the songs of various birds welcoming the new day.

At both the opening and closing of the day, God has provided heavenly music.

Summer Camp Develops Love of Nature

I just completed the first week of our summer camp here, during which I am teaching a nature course (what else?).

The children examined the canal system in leaves and the beauty of flower petals under a magnifying glass; toured and learned about our organic garden; and watched videos of remarkable animal habits and the grandeur of our planet. They pasted various seeds in their booklet, with the awareness of their potential, and learned of the condition of our planet and the drastic need for recycling its resources.

These children are our hope for the future, and the ecological spirituality given to them at camp may help steer them in the right direction to appreciate and seriously care for their Mother Earth.

Pickle Sale Stifled

It seems I've reached the last of the cucumbers for my pickle sales, which help support our center. The large amount of rain, coupled with the intense heat, has unfortunately stunted the growth of my crop.

I recall preserving almost two hundred pints of pickles during one season; these past weeks, I made fewer than fifty. The other farmers in the area are having problems also.

I read that cucumbers, originating in India, have been around for more than three thousand years. The Spaniards introduced them to Haiti in the fifteenth century. They became popular in North America in the mid-sixteenth century, and now China boasts of producing 60 percent of the world's cucumbers.

In England, some cucumbers grow as long as two feet; however, mine are less than a foot, which is fine. When I take a bite out of that crispy, juicy green veggie, I have no problem relating to the expression, "cool as a cucumber." Another of nature's treats.

The Versatile Eggplant

This morning I picked some of the last vegetables from our summer garden—eggplants.

Many Italian families reside in this area, and it's interesting to know that eggplants, which date back to the fifth century B.C., when they were first cultivated in China, were introduced in the Middle Ages to Italy, the country with which they have long been associated.

Prized for their beauty, as well as unique taste and texture, eggplants display such colors as purple, green, yellow, and white, and they range in size from that of a small tomato to a large zucchini. Health-wise, these vegetables are especially high in fiber and potassium. When laboratory animals with high cholesterol were given eggplant juice, their cholesterol was significantly reduced.

Our freezer is now pretty full of these parboiled treats, just waiting to be fried or smothered under red gravy. It's nice to know they hold an esteemed place in cuisines here and in many European countries.

Deer in Hiding

If I happen to return home after dark, I always turn on the car's bright lights so that when I face the woods I can count on seeing several pairs of eyes light up at the edge of the woods.

Our deer are very shy. The only time we see them is at night, when they come out to wander around the grounds, and when they see us they quickly head back to the woods.

When I visited a friend in Texas, I saw deer on her front lawn nonchalantly grazing away in broad sunlight. I couldn't believe it. In California I actually saw them grazing on a famous golf course—while players were out there. What's wrong with our deer?

It could be that ours have been hunted. During the deer season, I hear gunshots and know hunters are trespassing on our property, but I also know that if deer were not killed they would continue to multiply and eventually starve. My only fear is their suffering.

When I go camping with my family during Thanksgiving week, while the hunting season is open, we have to wear bright-colored vests, hopefully visible to the hunters, while hiking.

Once a deer fled though our campsite and jumped into the lake to avoid being shot. I was amazed at how he actually knew he was a target. Maybe our own deer have had this same experience, which deprives us of the joy of observing these beautiful, graceful creatures on our grounds.

A New Season of Colors

It seems to me there are a lot more colored leaves on our trees this year than in the past. Those maples, pears, and crepe myrtles are about to make me run off the road when I'm driving; they're so beautiful to view, and here our woods are filled with the multi-colored tallow leaves among the green pines and oaks.

I've discovered that those fall colors are present in the leaves throughout the spring and summer; the green chlorophyll just happens to be prominent during that time. When the water flow begins to decrease after the hot weather, the green disappears, and the yellow and orange pigments begin to show themselves.

When the food-producing sap containing sugar shows itself in the leaf, a red or purple color is displayed. Meanwhile, the needles and leaves of our numerous pines and oaks in this area continue to hold water and remain green throughout the year, since snow is an exciting oddity here.

Glory in the Morning

While driving down the highway last week I was a little depressed. I had just left two stores in which Christmas decorations already were displayed, and it was only the middle of September. What a way to cheapen a sacred holiday, trying to beat the other stores in capitalizing on the season.

What lifted my spirits was what I suddenly noticed next to the highway. It was morning, and all along the fence were clusters of blue morning glories. There they were, totally neglected, yet healthy and displaying a simple beauty to those who drove by.

I learned the flowers have a tolerance for poor, dry soils, which explains their presence and perseverance in many unexpected areas. Most of them close during the warm part of the day, but on a cloudy day they may last until night.

For a morning person like myself, they certainly glorify and celebrate the beginning of a new day for me. I have planted some along the back fence where I can see them in the early hours.

The Warmth of a Fireplace

A few days ago, while removing the hummingbird feeders from the trees for the winter, I spotted in the distance smoke rising from a home down our country road. It was the first I had seen since the weather had changed, and I was suddenly transported to the time I was twelve years old and we moved from New Orleans to the country across the lake.

We had no fireplace in the city, so when we drove up to our new home in the country, to which my father had gone ahead to prepare for our arrival, my first cause of excitement was the welcoming of that smoke spiraling from the chimney against a background of woods.

There's just something about a fireplace and woods. We had entered a new world, after that of concrete and traffic in the city. My love of nature had begun and has remained with me.

My life here in Rosaryville—after a busy life as a teacher, administrator, social worker, and missionary throughout the years—has been an answer to a prayer, as I am again surrounded by nature.

Bright Side of Winter

It's a little depressing to walk around the grounds and view the dead flowers, bushes, and plants that I so lovingly tended throughout the spring and summer months, Along with those feelings, however, is the anticipation of cutting them back in search of new life hidden beneath, and replanting.

I'm already collecting large cans from the kitchen with plans of starting off seedlings before transplanting them after the final frost. Also, raking up pine needles from all of our trees and bagging them gives me a lift, thinking of how they will protect the plants and beautify the gardens.

Speaking of beauty, the planet Venus is up there in the western sky every evening in all its glory—the first diamond in the sky—shining ever so brightly, especially during these winter months. Being out here with no artificial lights allows us to view millions of stars, which is really breathtaking.

So why shouldn't I have a positive attitude toward winter?

Hard Work Pays Off

At the end of each summer when our vegetable garden finally peters out, after a few months of planting, watering, hoeing, harvesting, chopping, shelling, bagging, freezing, pickling, and canning, it's time to bid adieu to it all and collapse. But when I look into the freezer packed full of squash, zucchini, corn, eggplants, beans, and okra, and at the shelves covered with dozens of pints of pickles, I know it was well worth the effort.

Each evening at sundown, as I made my way to the kitchen, hot, exhausted, and loaded down with buckets and bags full of produce, a hot shower was all I had on my mind. After having spent almost four years in Mexico working with the poor, my thoughts would then always turn to how they would appreciate having just a very small portion of that food I was carrying, and the blessing of having clean, hot, running water in their hovels.

My "burden" would be then lifted with those thoughts, and I would thank God for our many gifts.

Life After Death

A few weeks ago I forced myself to dig up my zinnias I had planted in the spring because they finally were dying. I had to accept the fact that after giving me countless beautiful flowers, with some stems growing to a height of over six feet, the flowers finally had completed their life span.

I took them into the woods, where I sadly deposited them and thanked them; and when I returned to the seemingly empty garden, I was met with a most pleasant surprise when I looked closely. Where the plants had stood, I noticed there were numerous small seedlings, as the flowers I had overlooked on the stalks had dried and sprinkled their seeds onto the ground.

Since cold weather doesn't arrive in this area until November, I dug up many of them and distributed them carefully and equally around the garden. I'm now awaiting another array of beauty and color while marveling at the miracle of new life that follows death.

Welcoming Cooler Days

During the past few weeks, Mother Nature has graciously bestowed on us unexpected cool mornings and evenings. At night I've been opening the window next to my bed to soak up that slight breeze coming in, along with the sounds of the crickets and frogs in the woods. It makes me want to stay awake just to enjoy it all.

At daybreak I've been eager to get out on the porch, often needing a light blanket, to experience the relief of the advent of this beautiful fall weather after a long, hot summer. Some of the most precious moments of these days have been those in my chair on the porch in the morning with my cup of coffee and Bible and my cat at my feet. Such peace.

We don't have the pleasure down south to witness many changing leaves, but just to sit and look out over the grounds bordered by deep woods of mainly evergreens is pleasing any time of year.

Tilting Earth Brings New Season

L ast week, when the first day of fall arrived, my thoughts turned to my camping gear in the closet and my family's annual Thanksgiving week in the Homochitto Forest of Mississippi.

Why this change of weather? Our northern hemisphere is now tilting away from the sun as it continues to revolve around it at a twenty-three-degree angle. People in the southern hemisphere, below the equator, are now observing new leaves on their trees and are planting, while our leaves are falling and our summer crops are in our freezers.

While I was leaving the dock over our lake earlier, after soaking up its beauty and peace for some time, I found it difficult to realize that while everything seems so motionless all round us, this planet on which we live is actually flying through space, circling the sun at a rate of seven thousand miles per hour, and completing its orbit in approximately 365 days. Also, while this is happening, the earth is making a complete turn on its axis every twenty-four hours.

Another thing: We automatically think we and everything around us are straight up, on top of the planet, when actually we're poking out on its side. Yet we're hanging on, thanks to gravity.

It's a little too much for my brain to comprehend.

Giving Thanks

That autumn harvest feast shared by the Plymouth colonists and Wampanoag Indians in 1621 is acknowledged today as the first Thanksgiving. And did those Pilgrims celebrate! I read that Chief Massasoit and his ninety men were fed and entertained for three days.

The only foods historians are sure were on their table were venison, wild turkey, corn, and probably lobster and seal. No mashed potatoes, cranberry sauce, nor pumpkin pie.

They didn't use forks—only spoons, knives, and their hands—but whatever way they did it, they celebrated, prayed, and expressed gratefulness for their blessings.

In 1782, the U.S. Congress issued a proclamation stating it was the "indispensable duty of all nations to give Almighty God praise for His goodness in general" and, "The practice of true and undefiled religion was the great foundation of public prosperity and national happiness."

Whatever has happened to that reverence of religion?

The Autumn Flower

Yesterday I was in a store where autumn decorations were being tacked up, and I suddenly had flashes of light jackets, cool breezes, colored leaves, and our family's annual camping trip. At a meeting I had attended the day before, we were all presented with small pots of chrysanthemums covered with dozens of buds just waiting to explode into gorgeous fall colors.

I was amazed to discover there are about thirty species of these autumn favorites, in the form of pompoms, quills, spiders, brushes, and buttons. Also, they are used in foods and medicines and to reduce indoor air pollution. When introduced into Japan in the eighth century, the emperor adopted the flower as his official seal. If chrysanthemums could speak, they could do lots of boasting.

I'll plant the one I just got as a gift near the birdbath in the garden—where the birds will keep it watered with all their splashing—and I can't wait for that explosion of beauty to happen. (Its little sign says it's purple.)

Conserving Resources at Night

After prayers and supper I enjoy sitting in my room, not watching television, but reading a good book. Being an avid reader, I grab every book of interest and information I can get my hands on, but when it gets dark my eyes get heavy and I'm ready for bed.

This is a problem, however, when daylight savings ends and it's dark by five-thirty. I look at the clock and think, "Oh, no! Five hours before bedtime. How will I stay awake?"

A lot more electricity is going to be used by all of us during these next few months of long nights. Those traditional incandescent light bulbs we've been using are, sadly, manufactured from coal, and the processing of this coal puts carbon, mercury, and other pollutants into the atmosphere.

Switching one 100-watt incandescent light bulb to a compact spiral fluorescent can cut the equivalent of one hundred pounds of coal. We have done this at our center so as to do our share in not depriving future generations of some of our planet's natural resources and clean air.

Our Rare Snow

During a recent winter, we experienced the excitement of a real snowfall—eight inches, in fact—a very rare happening down here. The blanket of snow covering our fields, shrines, and woods was awesome, and we snapped picture after picture.

It was actually the second snowfall I've ever witnessed, and I thought I was dreaming. Three months later, while visiting friends in Quebec, I unexpectedly encountered four feet of snow on the ground and light snowfalls during the day. My excitement puzzled the residents, who by then had had just about enough of it.

I read that the most snow ever to fall in one winter in the U.S. was in Washington State in 1998 to 1999, when a total of 1,140 inches fell.

I'm sure my excitement would decrease if I had to deal with blizzards, snow shovels, snow tires, slush, and the possibility of being trapped inside.

Slowing Down Time

Although the temperature has dropped into the low thirties this week, the blue sky and sunshine have drawn me to the beauty and peace of our two-acre lake.

Ordinarily, anyone's presence on the dock draws dozens of hopeful turtles from all directions. Today, however, there's no sign of one. I remember reading that with the coming of winter, turtles bury themselves in the mud under the water and stop breathing through their lungs. Because their life processes slow down so much, the small amount of oxygen absorbed through their skin is sufficient to keep them alive.

When I threw bread into the water, several huge catfish surfaced and seemed appreciative. (They're huge to me, but I read that some Eurasian catfish weigh more than six hundred pounds. Try taking that to a fish fry.) Their movements that day, however, seemed to be very slow compared to their normal, frantic grabbing of food.

They might be ready to die of old age. I'd catch a few before that happens, but I need someone to take them off the hook and hand them to me skinned and ready to grill.

Southern and Northern Winters

On these cold Louisiana days, while working outdoors on the grounds, I think of those up north who really know what cold weather is.

I recall reading the autobiography of a young woman, in which she writes of some of her family's winter experiences in Minnesota in the early 1900s. Her father had to get up several times during the night to go out into the snow and make the cows run so they wouldn't freeze to death. When they prepared to take a bath (not often), they would knock long icicles from the porch roof into a tub, in order to collect water to heat in the fireplace.

Most interesting of all to me was the way the author's mother dried their clothes. After washing them, she would hang them out on the line. The water on them would freeze immediately, and she would take a stick, knock all the ice off the clothes, and then take them off the line—cold, but dry.

I think I'd prefer to stay down south, where we can enjoy snow scenes on Christmas cards and, in rare cases, experience it firsthand for just a couple of hours.

A Horticultural Treasure

During these past few days, I've weeded and cut back my impatiens, vincas, roses, and lantana, but I'm not touching my unbelievably fragrant sweet olive tree, loaded with its tiny blossoms.

When my friend from South Carolina was getting ready to return home a few years ago and wanting to leave me a souvenir of her visit, she bought me the tree, which was very small at the time but now is about ten feet high. In mid-coastal areas such as ours, the trees can grow as tall as thirty feet.

Sweet olives are found in many old gardens in the South. They are long-lived trees that are infrequently bothered by pests and diseases. The aroma of their flowers can be enjoyed for several hundred feet. Long ago they often were planted near windows, which were open during the warm months, allowing their fragrance to permeate the homes.

There are times that you're not even aware of the tree nearby when that aroma hits you.

I wonder why they don't manufacture sweet olive perfume. It's bound to sell. I'd buy it.

Hurry Up, Spring

After several months of cold weather, I think we're all very ready for spring to arrive. I think, however, that possibly the robins, cardinals, and blue jays are downright impatient now. I have never seen so many of those colorful birds around here as I have during the past few weeks.

Yesterday I noticed that our Japanese magnolias are almost in full bloom, so I headed for the nearest nursery and bought two blueberry bushes to plant by the mandarin and fig trees. Then I headed across the road to collect some of our neighbor's cow manure to add to the decayed oak leaves I collected from the woods last week.

Even though I scraped some ice off the windshield of the car this morning, I've loaded up the golf cart with a shovel, spade, hoe, soil, and some nutrients, and I am raring to go with this gardening business.

The Excitement of a New Season

My favorite season has always been winter, and I've always dreaded seeing it come to an end. Feeling relief from the heat and humidity, wearing warm sweaters and scarves, and having energy for brisk walks have been really enjoyable these past years. This year, however, my knees are aching (is it age?), and I'm a little tired of looking at dead flowers everywhere. I will welcome the new life of spring.

While in a store yesterday, I saw potting soil, garden gloves, and packs of flower and vegetable seeds, and I think my heart skipped a beat. I went home and mapped out my summer gardens, and as I did, my excitement grew.

I'll dig up vinca seedlings from the seeds dropped in the fall and put them in small peat pots to transfer when the soil gets warmer. I won't dig up the zinnia seedlings; their mother plants grew over five feet tall, and all had to be supported. What a pain. I'm buying seeds for the dwarf zinnias this time.

I'll have the men who work on the grounds plow up the field for my vegetables and check the sprinklers I stored inside the barn, along with the fertilizers.

I can't believe I'm so excited about winter ending. I guess that comes with age.

The Exotic Camellia

This is the time of year I ride around the grounds of our retreat center in my golf cart, cutting camellias from our many bushes while oohing and aahing at their beauty and numerous varieties. I love to place them on tables in the dining room for those who come for retreats to help lift their spirits a little higher.

I don't know the life span of a camellia bush, but I imagine these bushes are the very same ones that I drove our gardener, old Sister Monica, to purchase at a nearby nursery back in the mid-1950s.

I read that there are about 250 species of camellias, and they were first cultivated in China and Japan, where tea is still made from the leaves of some of the species. They were eventually introduced to Europe and by the 1840s were at the height of their fashion, especially in Paris, and known as the "luxury flower."

Whether they are pink, red, white, pink tinged with purple, or red tinged with white, or have single or double leaves, each is a wonder to behold.

Sheltered Pets

I love cold weather, but what spoils my enjoyment of the fireplace, seasonal festivities, warm coats and blankets, and relief from this southern heat are the thoughts of animals that are not sheltered properly from the cold, especially during the nights. They didn't ask to be born, and their needs and sufferings are as real as ours.

My cats have well-insulated, cozy houses on the porch, safe from the cold north air. One morning I put my hand in one of the boxes to smooth out the blankets and felt something small, warm, and fuzzy 'way in the corner. I stooped down and looked in to find a baby possum, curled up and sound asleep. How he knew where there was a warm place, and how he climbed those high steps to get up on the porch, I don't know.

He was gone when I checked later, as they're night animals, but you've probably guessed that I set up another box for future cold nights. I haven't seen him since, however. Hopefully, his mother took better care of him after that.

Winter Joys

This past week, there was such a beautiful sight outside my window in the mornings, as the ground, trees, and bushes were covered with frost.

I've kept my three kitties, Timmy, Toby, and Ernie, inside with me during these cold nights, even though they have warm houses on the porch. With temperatures down in the twenties, I wasn't too sure about the protection I've provided.

Frost consists of tiny crystals of ice that grow out from solid surfaces after the surfaces have become colder than the surrounding air.

A hoar frost refers to the white crystals loosely deposited on exposed objects that make trees and bushes look like elderly white hair. The word "hoar" comes from Old English and is used as an adjective for showing signs of old age.

Hoar frosts actually can cause avalanches when they form on top of snow.

Even though I find it all beautiful, it's really not too much fun to have to scrape it off or throw cold water on my car window, especially when I'm in a big hurry. Beats shoveling snow, though.

Adapting to Temperatures

We've been greeted these cold mornings with frost on our grass, cars, and rooftops. I've even had to break up the ice in my cats' bowls on the porch. (I can just hear a Northerner saying, "Big deal.")

Cold weather increases my Christmas spirit, and I love it, but I can't get out of the back of my mind both the suffering of the poor and of animals without proper shelter.

Each fall, out come the three blanket-lined houses for my pets on the front porch, facing away from the north wind, and I can't help but worry about the animals in the woods behind my house.

There also are those creatures such as the goldfish out in the pond, who, like frogs, lizards, and others referred to as cold-blooded, have internal temperatures that vary considerably according to their surroundings.

They can contain four to ten enzyme systems that operate at different temperatures, unlike our bodies, which normally maintain the same temperature.

I can forget about the goldfish, I guess, but I still feel sorry for the possum, deer, and raccoons out there, especially on cold and rainy nights.

Displaying Christmas

It was in the fourth century that the pope specified December twenty-fifth as the official date of Christmas. The date chosen for this feast by the Church was the date on which the Romans had celebrated the birthday of their sun god, and the return of longer days of sunlight.

It wasn't until 1220, however, that St. Francis of Assisi was the first to have the idea to create a Nativity scene using live humans and animals. I don't believe there is a single Christian church or school today that does not reenact this sacred event each year.

One of our most serious and joyous activities here at the center at Christmastime is setting up our Nativity set outdoors for all who pass by to see. I can't help but wonder what's really being celebrated by those who only display Frosty, Rudolph, and Santa Claus, as lovable as those three are.

As the spirit of materialism increases at this time of year, we need to return to the simplicity of the star, cave, straw, animals, shepherds, hillsides, and the stillness of night, broken only by the sound of the music of angels, rather than the ringing of cash registers.

Simplify Christmas Giving

I always have believed the most fulfilling life is one that is simple and creative.

This philosophy led Henry Thoreau to Walden Pond, where he built his cabin and planted his garden in the woods in order to be immersed in nature. His journal has been read and admired by millions longing for such simplicity.

Whatever happened to those simple Christmases of the past about which we read and view on screen? Why do so few people now give gifts of homemade candles, tree ornaments, candy, cookies, Yule logs, and other creations from their hearts without fearing, "Is that enough?"

It upsets me to see so much hard-earned money spent this time of year, maybe with heavy heart, for electronic, mechanical, and other expensive articles, often out of a sense of obligation or competition.

I personally receive a great sense of joy during this season by creating handmade gifts, straight from the heart, such as a simple painted rock for a paperweight, a bookmark, a clay ashtray, or caramel corn.

What was simpler than that first Christmas?

Natural or Unnatural Trees?

There is never a question as to whether or not to have an artificial tree or a natural one in our community room for Christmas. During this festive season, how could we deprive ourselves of that fresh pine or spruce aroma from the woods filtering through our building?

Long before artificial trees were introduced, the first retail Christmas tree lot was opened in New York City in 1851, with trees brought from the Catskill Mountains. Five years later, President Franklin Pierce introduced the Christmas tree to the White House, and the first national tree was lighted in 1923 on the White House lawn by President Calvin Coolidge.

Each year, an estimated 40 to 45 million Christmas trees are planted in North America. These tree farms support complex ecosystems, absorb carbon dioxide, send oxygen into the air, and return nutrients to the earth through decomposition.

Many of our natural resources are used to create artificial trees; also, they create dangerous dioxins in the manufacturing process and are nonbiodegradable.

How can there be a question as to what trees should grace our homes at this time of year?

English Customs

I love the fact that the English have given us many Christmas traditions derived from nature, such as the display of mistletoe, holly, ivy, and Yule logs in our homes.

We can't bring enough nature inside at this time of year. Together, we string garlands of pine, caught up with red ribbons, along the staircases and mantelpieces. The refectory has Yule logs with candles on the tables, and, of course, adorning our community room, sits the tree in all its glory, with the humble crèche below.

Although the custom of cutting a tree in the woods and taking it into the house to decorate originated in Germany, it was Prince Albert, husband of Queen Victoria, who popularized the Christmas tree in England by introducing one to the royal household and decorating it with candles in 1841.

Other English traditions are the small groups of carolers who go from house to house singing carols, many of which were written in England. Another custom is the serving of flaming plum pudding at the Christmas meal, after their Father Christmas has brought gifts for the family.

By the way, I read that instead of leaving cookies and milk for Father Christmas when he is depositing gifts, the English leave him brandy and mincemeat pie, along with a carrot and water for the reindeer.

A generous lot.

Origin of the Christmas Tree

The decorated Christmas tree can be traced back to the ancient Romans who, during their winter festival in honor of the god of agriculture, adorned trees with small pieces of shiny metal.

Late in the Middle Ages, the Germans began placing evergreen trees inside their homes to show their hope in the forthcoming spring, and it is believed that it was Martin Luther who first placed lighted candles on them to represent the light of Christ.

In America, trees bearing candles were introduced by the German Moravian Church in Bethlehem, Pennsylvania, on Christmas of 1747, and it is from them that we get many of this season's customs, songs, images of Santa, and handblown glass ornaments.

When we were children, we got our first glimpse of the family tree on Christmas morning, as Christ's birth had been celebrated a few hours before at midnight. At our retreat center, however, we anticipate and celebrate this event a few days early in order to stretch out the season a little longer.

Christmas Mistletoe

When I was twelve years old, my family moved from New Orleans to a wooded area north of the lake into a house completely surrounded by trees.

During the Christmas season, I had seen mistletoe hung in houses and sold in stores but didn't know its origin until my brother pointed out to me the bushes in the trees right above us. He would get out his rifle and shoot off some of the branches of the bushes, and we would use red ribbons to tie together small clusters containing the white berries to hang above the doorways in the house.

As we know, it's an ancient Christmas custom for a man and woman to kiss under a sprig of mistletoe. In the past, each time the man kissed the woman he would pluck off a berry, and when they were all gone, he would lose his privilege.

After the birds have eaten the berries off the bushes in the trees, the berries go through their digestive systems, and if the droppings fall on a suitable part of a tree, germination of another mistletoe bush will take place.

The word "mistle" is the Anglo-Saxon word for "dung," and "tan" or "toe" is the word for "twig," giving us the words "dung on a twig." But let's not think about that while the kissing is going on.

Hang On to That Tree

Today, December twenty-fifth, we celebrate the first day of Christmas. Yes, the first: not the one and only.

I notice there are lots of pear trees around; however, I'm not sure the true loves of those reading this will present them with a partridge.

We are told the first visitors to the newborn baby Jesus in the stable were lowly shepherds. This is an indication of Jesus' love for the poor and simple. However, twelve days later, the Church celebrates the arrival of three kings with costly gifts—an indication of the dignity and royalty of the child.

Anyway, don't be too much in a hurry to throw that tree out, since we continue to celebrate Christmas for those twelve days between the Nativity and Kings Day on January sixth.

New Year's Traditions

The celebration of a new year is the oldest of all holidays, first observed in ancient Babylon on an unknown date about four thousand years ago.

Two thousand years later, the New Year began to be celebrated on the first day of spring—a logical time to start, as it was the season of rebirth.

In 153 A.D., the Romans declared January first the beginning of the New Year and celebrated it for eleven days. The Christians saw this as paganism and began having their own religious observances on that day.

The Scottish song "Auld Lang Syne," which means "the good old days," usually is sung at the stroke of midnight, along with the toasting of champagne. An old Roman custom was to place a piece of toast in the wine to absorb some of its acidity—thus, the word "toasting."

For good luck during the year ahead, the custom of eating black-eyed peas began, and for prosperity, cabbage, representing paper currency, was eaten.

Let's not forget the custom of those resolutions such as losing weight, giving up smoking, and exercising more. Let's add having a greater appreciation of others, our remarkable planet, and their creator.

New Season Begins

On the sixth of January, Twelfth Night is celebrated on a large scale, especially in New Orleans, as the carnival season opens.

Twelfth Night also is known as Kings Day, and bakeries throughout the New Orleans area get busy producing numerous King Cakes. This continues until Mardi Gras day, when King Cake parties are held in homes.

Not to put a damper on things, but as the celebrations continue and we continue to overeat, it would be good for us to be aware of the fact that two-thirds of the U.S. population is overweight, while two-thirds of the world goes hungry.

I read that Americans spend about $42 billion a year on weight-loss products and programs. There's something wrong with this picture.

Other suggested New Year's resolutions: Let's plant more vegetable gardens; cut back on fast foods and overeating, which are ruining our health; and share our wealth with those less fortunate.

To Be Continued

Before a new year begins, the media always gets busy publishing facts of personalities and events that have stirred up interest and made a difference during the past year.

Most of us don't make it into that limelight, but then what difference does that make, as long as we're living as we should in loving communion with God's creations, and therefore immersed in that "peace which the world cannot give"?

Some, however, live their lives on the surface of things, unaware of the beauties of nature with which we have been gifted as benefactors of this planet so in need of maintenance and protection.

As serious caretakers of our animals and natural resources, we can count ourselves among those giants who continue to make this world a better place while continuing God's work of creation.

Our Precious Trees

I get very upset every time I purchase something in a store and am given a receipt that is two, three, or four times the length it should be.

The top part contains the amount of purchase, and below that is a list of advertisements, sales offers, and God-knows-what. My remarks concerning wasted paper haven't changed a thing, it seems.

Once at home, most people probably throw those receipts in the trash, to be counted among the 85 million tons of paper discarded annually. When left to decompose in landfills, paper gives off methane, a gas twenty-three times more potent than carbon dioxide. Millions of trees are being harvested unnecessarily as a result of this indifference and waste.

Considered the "lungs of the earth," constantly sending oxygen and water into the air, our precious trees are rapidly disappearing from our planet.

When purchasing paper, let's look for that which has been recycled. For every twenty-five pounds, or five reams, of recycled paper purchased, 33,485,208 trees are saved. Locate your nearest recycling bin.

The New Life of Spring

That beautiful first full moon of spring on Thursday evening ushered in, as it always does, the Passover and Easter seasons.

New life abounds everywhere. The birds around here are especially excited about it all as they rush here and there toward their nests carrying big, fat worms in their beaks for their babies. Colorful butterflies are emerging and flying free from their life in dark cocoons, spun when they were unsightly caterpillars.

In an effort to save some of my flowers last week, I hosed an ant nest, only to see lots of those white eggs left behind. I saw the adult ants heading back weakly, picking the eggs up to carry them off to safety and their new life. Talk about my feeling guilty!

Then there are the crops. It was probably too wet for the farmers who plant on Good Friday, but with those seedlings in the ground, we all will be anticipating the miraculous growth that will provide us with a variety of food.

Let's all be aware of the miracles surrounding us, especially at this time of year.